What we eat when we eat alone

What we eat
when we eat
alone

Deborah Madison
and Patrick McFarlin

Art by Patrick McFarlin

GIBBS SMITH
TO ENRICH AND INSPIRE HUMANKIND
Salt Lake City | Charleston | Santa Fe | Santa Barbara

First Edition
13 12 11 10 09   10 9 8 7 6 5 4 3 2 1

Published by
Gibbs Smith
P.O. Box 667
Layton, Utah 84041

1.800.835.4993 orders
www.gibbs-smith.com

Designed and produced by Patrick McFarlin
Printed and bound in the United States
Gibbs Smith books are printed on either recycled, 100% post-consumer waste, FSC-certified papers
or on paper produced from a 100% certified sustainable forest/controlled wood source.

Library of Congress Cataloging-in-Publication Data

Madison, Deborah.
What we eat when we eat alone / Deborah Madison and Patrick McFarlin ;
illustrations by Patrick McFarlin. — 1st ed.
p. cm.
ISBN-13: 978-1-4236-0496-9
ISBN-10: 1-4236-0496-2
1. Cookery for one. I. McFarlin, Patrick. II. Title.
TX652.M2255 2009
641.5'61—dc22
2008035669

This book is dedicated to all who find themselves
alone at the table.
May your solitary meals be delicious and
the company just as good.

CONTENTS

CHAPTER 1

What We Eat When We Eat Alone

"It seems to me that eating alone is about having something satisfying, like all corn and tomatoes, without having to follow the rules the way you do when you have to consider someone else. Though I suppose that if I ate alone all the time, I'd be the opposite, making swell little meals in a committed way."

—Fran McCullough, *cookbook author*

FOR A NUMBER OF YEARS we traveled frequently to Mediterranean countries at the invitation of Oldways Preservation and Trust. During these eye-opening—and mouth-opening—journeys, we met many producers and tasted their olive oils, wine, ouzo, breads, cheeses, and countless other foods made according to ancient ways. There were enough chefs, importers, scholars, and food writers to fill a couple of busses on each of these trips, and inevitably there were long rides across dry lands that afforded hours for conversation. On one of those trips, artist Patrick McFarlin found his amusement not in watching a blindfolded camel in a Tunisian village pulling a stone over rancid olives to press a very singular-tasting oil, but in asking people what they cooked for themselves when they ate alone.

"I started to inquire into the habits of other people's private culinary lives on these trips," Patrick explains. "The research was entirely unscientific. I simply asked people about their behind-closed-doors food practices. Some were ordinary, some quirky, and others credible and civilized."

People rolled into Patrick's research inquiries as if they were on an afternoon televised exposé—throwing open the secrets of their cloistered cupboards and refrigerators.

The stories people had stashed up their sleeves were so surprising that we continued asking others on a regular basis what they eat when they eat alone—and writing down their answers. What emerged is a portrait of human behavior sprung free from conventions, a secret life of consumption born out of the temporary freedom—or burden, for some—of being alone. There are foods that are so utterly idiosyncratic that they would never, ever, be shared with another, and there are some very ambitious undertakings. "I pour sardine juice onto cottage cheese while standing on one foot in front of the refrigerator, not

putting down the other foot because there's been a meat leak from the vegetable drawer," said one shamelessly, while another admitted to eating while lying on the couch with a newspaper spread over the chest to catch any drips. But there are lots of meals cobbled together during football halftimes that have real possibilities, dishes that can be worked into recipes for tasty and fairly easy-to-make everyday kinds of foods.

Even after our travels, people have continued to speak to us with enthusiasm and candor about their exploits in the realm of cooking for one. Their revelations have made us see how many possibilities there are for feeding ourselves, possibilities that lie well outside the borders of what usually passes for normal, let alone "right." When we eat alone we often break all the rules surrounding not only what to eat but when to eat and even where. And this is true regardless of what we know about cooking or about what makes a proper meal. As writer Fran McCullough says, solo meals can be all corn and tomatoes if that's what you like. Solo meals are different, surprising, and they can also be funny, but sometimes predictable.

Some men cook exceptionally well for themselves—roasting meats, opening fine bottles of wine as well as a book, and enjoying their own company, while others are happy eating a sandwich at the kitchen counter. Women, who especially enjoy being liberated from the routine of cooking for others, often see solo dining as an opportunity to eat not only what they want ("a bowl of oatmeal with *fleur de sel*" says one who is otherwise quite a sophisticated cook), but whenever and wherever. Do we eat on the couch or set a proper place for ourselves? Sip soup at our computers or wander around talking on the phone while eating? We do all of these things and more when there's no one watching and expecting us to do otherwise.

There's tremendous variety in the foods we turn to when we're alone—snacks, old standbys, adventurous dishes, expensive cuts of meat, or the single vegetable menu. But regardless of the particulars, the minute we include even one other person at the table, everything changes. Our cooking can become more joyful and exuberant, or it can become freighted with such things as the hope of seduction, intentions to nourish, annoyance about having to cook or clean up, and all the other emotions, good and less so, associated with cooking and feeding others.

What We Eat When We Eat Alone is hardly meant to be a definitive study of human behavior. Rather, we've simply been chatting with friends and strangers about the art—or chore—of feeding ourselves. The solo eating we're thinking about doesn't have to do with dashing bachelors and martini suppers, but with any of us who take meals alone, who have times when we cook and eat without another person in mind. We have interviewed people who share our worlds—other cooks, farmers, artists, writers—as well as random others we've sat next to at a concert or on a bus to the airport, our friends' elderly parents or their twenty-year-olds, for age is no barrier to the need for the occasional solo meal.

ABOUT THE RECIPES

After cooking many of the dishes people said they made for themselves—and taking some liberties with them—we've concluded that what most people want is to be involved in preparing their meals, but to a limited extent only. And this is true whether they are food professionals or work at something else entirely. While some true food maniacs are delighted to spend a few hours making sausage for themselves or boning and stuffing a chicken, most of us want a much smaller investment of time when it comes to dinner. We're simply not going to make lasagna from scratch, as appealing as homemade lasagna might be, but we will happily wash, chop, and cook something—as long as it doesn't go on too long. And it's quite impressive what you can accomplish in a short time without resorting to frozen or processed foods, microwaves, or takeout. After all, when it's just for one person, not four or six, there's that much less to do.

Cooking for one, it turns out, is a lot of fun, because recipes suggest rather than dictate, and that's because cooking for oneself is really about cooking by eye, deciding how much of this or that ingredient pleases you, or if you want to build in leftovers or not. We suspect that if you want to undertake a particular dish using special ingredients and techniques and all, you will go to a reliable cookbook to find out how. But here, measurements need not always be exact and the success of a recipe doesn't depend on too much precision or adherence to someone else's standards. More than ever, the specific shapes these recipes take ultimately depend on your likes, dislikes, and the state of your pantry.

Think about short pasta with cauliflower for example. You might ask yourself, for starters, do you love, or even like, cauliflower? Do you want only a small amount of pasta in proportion to the vegetable or the other way around? Do you eat like a bird or feed like a lion? Avoid oil or embrace it? I happen to love a lot of cauliflower and want just a few noodles for textural contrast when I make this dish, but you might want a full 4-ounce serving of pasta decorated with just a few cauliflower tidbits. Both are entirely legitimate approaches, and when you're alone in your kitchen, there's no need to explain or defend the choices you've made.

A friend who read our manuscript early on scrawled at the bottom of one chapter, "All these recipes are Southwestern!" And although we live in New Mexico, this has pretty much nothing to do with the preponderance of such recipes in the book. It surprised us, too, how often people turned to some combination of chiles, tortillas, salsa, and cheese as solutions to what to eat when alone. It's as if these are the new American foods and flavors, and particularly satisfying ones at that. And they have little to do with where one lives. Minnesota, Washington, New York, California—the Southwest is everywhere.

We were also stuck by how many times people called for "good olive oil." In a way this wasn't too surprising since quite a few of those Patrick interviewed originally were on these trips to countries where olive oil plays a major role. But others called for good olive oil too. It's clear that something has shifted in our food culture, that you can live in Arkansas and never have been to Italy and still be sure you're going to cook only with "good olive oil."

Good olive oil aside, we've given a lot of these idiosyncratic meals and menus a try. Of course there are those down and dirty dishes that can't be translated or shared but that do horrify and amuse, but then there are some solo eating practices that can, with a twist here and a knock there, be turned into quite usable recipes. Finally, there are quite a few dishes that are really very good and definitely worthy of a recipe, and we want to share the best ones with you. Who can, after all, argue with the goodness of a meal consisting of a roast leg of lamb and a bottle of old-vine Zinfandel? Why, a vegetarian, of course! But what vegetarian can argue with warm polenta smothered with wild mushrooms or braised greens?

Everyone eats alone at one time or another. There are those

periods of solo eating that ensue when we're young and out in the world for the first time, again when we're old, and sometimes during the years in between when we find ourselves without a partner to eat with. But during those years that we are living with partners and children, there are also invariably times when we find ourselves eating alone, cooking for just ourselves and no one else. It may be only for a single day, perhaps a weekend, or possibly a week or more that we'll find ourselves no longer constrained by what others expect for dinner or what time it should take place.

Whenever these moments occur and however long they last, they present us with the opportunity to keep our own best company.

When it comes to where we eat, the bed is a zone that's highly frowned upon but also indulged. *On* the bed is permissible, but never *in* bed, insist more than a few women.

"The thought of eating in bed is sort of creepy," muses Maureen Callahan, "but that might have something to do with growing up in Florida. The thought of those big bugs marching up for a crumb or two . . . ooh! It gives me the willies!"

Then again, there are exceptions. Another woman says, "I make a tray of cold, sliced chicken breast, fruit, and cheese, take it to bed, and get right under the covers. I read, the cat purrs, and we're both happy. I love this time to myself."

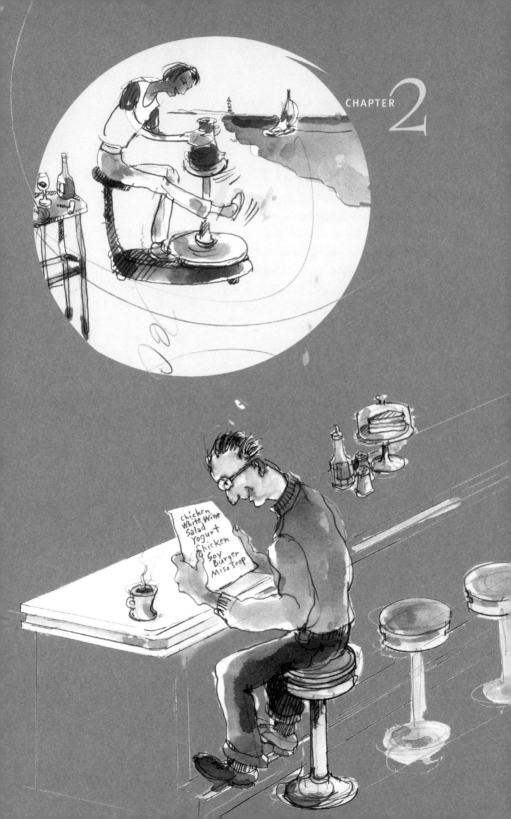

CHAPTER 2

The Gestalt of Eating
Men and Women at the Table

"This is a virtual world war of food and drink!"
—Milton Glaser

AT A GRAPHIC ARTS WORKSHOP held at the New York School for Visual Arts in the early eighties, long before our first trip to Spain with a group of writers and chefs, Patrick was introduced to the gestalt of eating. An unlikely place, you might be thinking. "But," Patrick says, "considering the workshop was taught by Milton Glaser, a whole-systems kind of guy, it makes sense. In a letter inviting us to New York, he outlined the following assignment:

> The week preceding the class, I'd like you to keep an exact record of everything you eat and drink, including size of portion and time eaten. Organize this information on an $8\frac{1}{2}$ x 11-inch sheet(s) of paper without signing or indicating in any way your authorship. Keep it with you in class. At one point I'll ask for it.

"On the third day, Glaser collected all the assignments, shuffled them, and passed them out. Then he gave us the real assignment.

Tonight after class, read the record of food and drink I've given you. Then read it again. Keep reading it until an image of the author emerges. Make a portrait of the person and mount it on illustration board. Then write a one-page description of your subject's typical day.

"It's astonishing how much a diet journal reveals. The size and portion part of the record tells as much about the person as the kinds of food and drink, as does the time one eats," Patrick observed.

"The question of what sex I was dealing with became clear immediately. I stationed myself in a coffee shop, document in hand. With the first cup I nailed it. Clearly this was the record of a woman. This was not a cheeseburger-cheeseburger-cheeseburger diet. There were too many chicken and white wine combos for a man. Occasionally a girl will eat a chili dog, but a man will go to the dogs four times a week. I read it over and over and, sure enough, a character walked into my imagination."

While we all eat many of the same foods, men and women differ in the ways they eat in a fairly predictable way, though not entirely. There are always those pesky exceptions that make life interesting, for men and women can change places and do so regularly. While I will share a steak with Patrick on occasion, I have never entertained the possibility that I might pick up one for myself when he's out of town. Other women, when asked, have told us the same thing. But then, a slender young woman quietly revealed that she loves to have a steak when her boyfriend is away.

"The fattier the better," she confides.

Still, we haven't met the woman yet who will eat a steak three times a week. She will, however, eat from a pot of soup night after night. A man might eat a hamburger twice a day, but not a woman. A woman will eat too much and have an Alka-Seltzer evening once in a while. A guy, however, will settle in and make a habit of eating large quantities of food, as if it proves something about his maleness. A guy might swig whisky between bites of food and a woman might prefer white wine. But if she does have a whisky, she's probably sipping, not swigging.

To boldly generalize, men are simple and women are complex when it comes to food. Women's choices are often more thought out, whereas men are "I like this and that's what I eat." Over and over again.

If you cook in a restaurant, you'll notice that women tend to be more adventurous about what they order, and that they like to share their plates with others so that they can taste everything. Men, more often, like to know that a certain dish they've grown accustomed to eating will always be there for them. And as for taking tastes off others' plates? Well, that's just not something most men are eager to do.

"We're predictable and consistent," Patrick says, speaking for men in general. "We have the same kind of breakfast five times a week, the same hamburger for lunch, similar dinner themes, and many identical full meals."

And we're not just talking about gonzo guys. Refined men like repetition, too. Richard McCarthy, who runs the Crescent City farmers markets, says that when it comes to cooking during the rare moments he's home alone, he's a "bit of a pomp-and-circumstance cook," by which he means many pots and pans are involved. "Even at the worst of times I don't open a can."

What comes to mind for Richard are such dishes as sliced Creole tomatoes with cracked black pepper and hard cheese, mushroom omelets, sautéed kale with sesame oil and rice vinegar, bushels of fava beans, and buckets of beets. Not your usual solo male menu, in part because Richard is a vegetarian.

"But at heart," he says, "I'm also a peasant. I'd happily eat the same foods for days. If left to my own devices, probably I would."

Women are less predictable. On their own, they eat when they feel like it, have ice cream for dinner, or, if they've had wine and cheese in the late afternoon, they might skip dinner altogether. Then again, they might get a wild hair and cook a big greasy lamb chop. You just never know.

One thing we do know is that if women cook all the time for others, they're not too inclined to get out the pots and pans and cook for themselves. Hence the repast of corn on the cob only, or a feast of frozen Tater Tots. But there are some crossover foods.

Frito pie is something that reads like a guy dish, but this recipe comes from a woman. First, some background. Frito pie is a culinary icon in Santa Fe, where we live. You find it at flea markets, ball games, and fairs, and Woolworth's used to sell Frito pie when they still had a store on the plaza. They'd open a bag of Fritos and ladle chili on top and you'd eat it right out of the bag. It made a funky but good (as in tasty, not good for you), cheap meal. Now you can get a Frito pie around the corner at the Plaza Café or out at Harry's Roadhouse, a bit fancier and more expensive, but still good (as in tasty, but better for you.) The bag has been sacrificed and the new Frito pie is served on a plate. It might be vegetarian, and it will include some salady toppings. But here's the version suggested by one of our female eaters, an East Coast gal.

"Use Hormel beans!" she commands. "Heat them in the microwave. Add Frank's RedHot, a buffalo-wing sauce. Put Fritos on a plate and pour the beans over them. Or, just forget the chili. Melt cheese over Fritos in a toaster oven for Frito nachos."

On the other hand, here's a conscientious dish that really does sound more like something a woman would eat. But this man's trade secret for solo eating comes from a transplanted American writer who's lived in England long enough to have acquired an accent. Here's what he does for dinner.

"I open a tub of cottage cheese and eat it with a puffed rice biscuit, cucumber, and tomato with salt and pepper." If you'd put it on a plate, you'd have a nice little diety dinner, improved with a drizzle of good oil and freshly ground pepper, plus a clump of watercress.

Even with our often correct stereotypes of how men and women eat, Patrick's own record of food and drink for the Glazer assignment was schizoid enough that it probably had a confusing effect on the classmate who received it.

"At the time, I was a bachelor and a vegetarian," Patrick says. "I was eating girly food when I wrote my menu—salads, tofu, things like that. My menu contrasted lunches constructed at Wendy's salad bars with evenings spent pitting swigs of whisky against avocado tacos. Glaser randomly chose my journal to read out loud, including all the jumps from sprouts to swigs of scotch."

"This is a virtual world war of food and drink!" Glaser announced to the class.

And indeed, eating solo can resemble eating in the trenches. But then again, it can be an opportunity to take the time to develop a meal, slowly savor it, and drink more wine than usual, as many of our interviewees have confided.

There is an underlying current that hints at self-deprecation when eating alone, particularly among women who, far more frequently than men, admit that when it's just them they're feeding they don't feel that they deserve the effort they'd expend for another.

"I'd like to say that I spend the afternoon preparing a flavorful, tender braise for myself," writes one woman, "but in truth, I'd never spend my time and effort for my own gratification. That degree of commitment is reserved for meals to be shared."

One man admitted that it was just too hard to work up enough enthusiasm for his own meals to even bother, and another, my dentist, says flatly, "It's just not worth eating when I'm alone." Still there's the cop who, between hotdog dinners, makes a vat of Bolognese sauce, taking no shortcuts to do so, or the farmer who comes to the end of his day with a harvest of vegetables that becomes his ratatouille—both good, self-respecting approaches.

When it comes to where we eat, what most men revealed was right in line with clichéd expectations—they do eat in such places as over the sink, in front of the fridge, while pacing around, and even lying on the couch. Of course there are also plenty of civilized men who eat at tables or seated in armchairs. Women also confessed to eating at the stove or leaning against the counter, and one woman described tearing apart a roasted chicken with such gusto while leaning over the sink that it was just about frightening!

Men, however, don't eat on the bed, or in it, while the bed seems to be a permissible dining area for women. Nor do men curl up with a cup of cocoa on the couch, and they don't tend to qualify their answers the way women do. Most of the women we spoke with discussed their areas of degustation with such qualitative words as *never* and *always*. "I always eat at the table. I would never eat in bed. I never watch television; I never watch for more than an hour; I only watch the news and that while sitting on the edge of the bed."

A man wouldn't say things like that. Funny. They just eat where they wish. End of story.

When it comes to shopping, it looks like men hunt and women gather. Other couples share our experience. When I casually say to Patrick, "Why don't you pick out some vegetables that look good to you while you're at the market," he blanches, as if I've asked him to do something that's painfully difficult.  We've talked about this. I know he has his favorite vegetables that I forget to buy, like spinach, but cruising the produce aisle is not a pleasing notion for him. "I dread having to go over to the vegetable counter and study all those options," he says. "I just want to get in and get out." He seldom comes home with impulse items other than a bottle of wine.

I, on the other hand, and most women I know, if we're not in a serious rush, tend to stroll through the market and consider what we see, deciding as we go what we want to eat and what we want to cook, or what special treat those we are cooking for might like. We may be sparked by something new, inspired by something that looks especially fresh, or curious about pursuing a new recipe. Or maybe we just have some little craving to satisfy. Certainly we almost always buy more than whatever is on our list, that is, if we have a list.

One last thought before we go on to some recipes suitable for men or women eating alone. In researching this book, we noticed that men and women tend to differ when it comes to the language of cooking. In the process of revealing the culinary underbelly of friends and strangers, we discovered that men predictably use a pretty aggressive vocabulary when describing their kitchen actions. They slam tortillas into skillets, break up stuff, smash foods, and stick them in whatever, the last verb being a favorite. Women, we found, tend to dice, sprinkle, and stir until a certain thing happens. They're generally more civilized. They cook. Never do they "take some vegetable and stick it in some pasta." But then again, I just read the words of a gorgeous woman featured in *Esquire* magazine who says she stabs the hell out of steak—really stabs it. But that's just to make it tender. Then she cooks it over a low, gentle heat, which a man probably wouldn't do.

A ripe avocado diced and tossed with salsa and then tucked into soft corn tortillas is a fundamental food. Have it with the tomatillo salsa (page 73), salsa fresca (page 77), or whatever your favorite hot sauce happens to be. Fresh cilantro is always welcome, of course.

2 corn tortillas

½ avocado, cut into chunks

salsa, your choice

a few cherry tomatoes, halved

salt

crumbled Cotija, grated Muenster, and/or Jack cheese

chopped cilantro

For cheese, use a melting Muenster or Monterey Jack, accented with crumbles of Cotija, a dry, sharp Mexican cheese. And don't feel you have to eat an entire avocado at once. You don't. If you have a half left, just put it in a waxed paper sandwich bag and refrigerate for the next day. You might want to slice off any discolored surfaces, but otherwise, it will be fine.

1. Put the corn tortillas in a hot skillet without any oil over medium-high heat. Turn them occasionally to warm them throughout while you make the filling.

2. Mix the avocado with a few spoonfuls of salsa and the cherry tomatoes. Season with a pinch or two of salt.

3. When the tortillas are hot and soft, cover them with the cheese or cheeses, let melt a little, then spoon the avocado on half of each one, add the cilantro, fold, and eat. That's it.

A DIETY COTTAGE CHEESE PLATE WITH WATERCRESS AND CUCUMBERS

You can use any or all kinds of cucumbers—lemon cukes with their bright yellow skins, skinny Persian cucumbers, or scalloped Armenians. Mixing chopped watercress into the cottage cheese flecks it with bits of green and makes it nicely peppered. I like the integrated flavors, but leave them separate if you prefer. Spoon the cottage cheese on your toast and add cucumbers, or eat everything separately.

a 3- or 4-inch length of cucumber
a handful of watercress,
   plus a few sprigs
cottage cheese, your favorite style
1 ripe tomato, cut into
   wedges or rounds
olive oil
salt and pepper
toast, rice cakes, or crackers

1. Slice as much cucumber as you want to eat. Should you have a tender-skinned cucumber from the farmers market, don't bother to peel it. Do peel a cucumber if it's been waxed.

2. Set aside the sprigs of watercress. Break off and discard the tougher stems of the rest, then chop finely. Stir the watercress into the cottage cheese. Mound the cottage cheese onto a plate and surround it with the cucumbers and tomatoes. Drizzle a little olive oil over all, then add a pinch of salt and freshly ground pepper.

3. Tuck the toast, rice cakes, or crackers onto the plate. Add those watercress sprigs you set aside to make the plate pretty.

TOMATO SALAD WITH BLACK PEPPER AND HARD CHEESE

Whether you've procured tomatoes from your own garden or someone else's via the farmers market, a plate of colorful heirloom or Creole tomatoes is a sure and festive bet for any eater. A tomato salad might be dinner for a light eater, but it also makes a fine accompaniment to roast chicken (page 214), skillet cheese (page 225), and egg dishes of all kinds. Don't be afraid to be generous, because you can cook any leftover tomato into a tangy little sauce in just a few minutes. It may not yield much, but it will be delicious stirred into an omelet or frittata.

a scant pound of heirloom tomatoes, including some of the tiny "fruit" varieties

2 scallions, finely sliced, including a bit of the greens

2 teaspoons red wine vinegar or an herbal white vinegar

salt and pepper

2 tablespoons of your best olive oil

fresh herbs, such as basil, lovage leaves, or dill, torn or slivered

hard cheese, such as aged goat, Gouda, or Asiago, shaved

good crusty bread

Slice the larger tomatoes into rounds and lay them on a dinner plate. Halve the smaller fruit tomatoes (cherry and plum varieties) and scatter them over the others. Combine the scallions in a small bowl with the vinegar and a few pinches of salt. Whisk in the olive oil. Pour the dressing over the tomatoes and grind plenty of pepper over all. Tear the herbs over the top and finish with thin shavings of hard cheese. Serve with good crusty bread.

Here's a fast meaty sandwich or two for a vegetarian. Generally it's easier to have leftover cooked tofu than half a piece floating in its carton, but in this case, it's such a snap to cook the tofu, you might as well leave any extra in the carton—covered with cold water. Try not to forget about it, and use it within a few days.

½ carton firm tofu, drained

oil for the pan

splash of Worcestershire sauce

salt and pepper

toast for 1 or 2 sandwiches

mustard, horseradish, and mayonnaise

tomatoes in season, sliced

sauerkraut

1. Slice the tofu crosswise into 4 pieces, each about ½ inch thick. Blot well with paper towels.

2. Heat an 8 or 10-inch cast-iron or nonstick skillet. Brush it with oil and add the tofu. Cook over medium-high heat until golden, about 6 minutes on each side. Douse with Worcestershire sauce, turn the tofu once, and continue cooking until the tofu is glazed and the sauce has evaporated. Season with salt and plenty of freshly ground pepper.

3. Make the toast. Slather it with mustard, horseradish, and mayonnaise, add the tofu and sliced tomato, cut the sandwich in half, and serve with a mound of sauerkraut on the side.

STEAMED KALE WITH SESAME OIL
AND RICE WINE VINEGAR

It's the dark roasted sesame oil and delicate vinegar that makes this kale so very good.

Sprinkle toasted sesame seeds over the kale, or season with or gomashio (a Japanese condiment of toasted ground sesame seeds and salt) before serving.

1 bunch curly green kale

2 to 3 teaspoons dark sesame oil, to taste

2 teaspoons rice wine vinegar, to taste

salt

red pepper flakes

toasted sesame seeds* or gomashio

1. Slice or pull the kale leaves off of the stems. Throw the stems away, as they will never become tender, and then wash the leaves. Steam the kale over boiling water until it is tender, about 12 minutes. Take a taste to make sure and then dump the cooked kale into a bowl.

2. Toss the kale with sesame oil and vinegar to taste, then season with salt and a few pinches of red pepper flakes. Toss again with a teaspoon or two of toasted sesame seeds, or serve with gomashio.

---

*To toast sesame seeds, put them in a dry skillet over medium heat. Once the pan becomes hot, start stirring or flipping the sesame seeds until they become golden, then remove from heat and turn them onto a plate immediately so that they don't keep cooking in the heat of the pan.

FRITO PIE NEW MEXICAN STYLE

There's the canned *chili con carne* poured into the bag of Fritos, the Frito pie with its Hormel beans and Frank's RedHot, then there's this New Mexican version, which consists of pure red chile, local beef, pinto beans, Fritos, and a salady topping. Except for the Fritos, this is actually a pretty healthful meal (and tortilla chips make a fine replacement for Fritos). It also makes people smile.

3 or 4 long red New Mexican chile pods with stems

salt

a few drops vinegar, if needed

1 tablespoon oil

1 pound ground beef or bison

½ cup or more cooked pinto beans per serving (page 78)

a small handful Fritos or tortilla chips

grated Cheddar cheese

finely slivered Romaine lettuce, 1 diced tomato, chopped cilantro, diced onion, and pickled onion rings (page 95) or scallions to finish

It is not, however, an instant meal, because you've got to cook the beans (unless they're canned), the chiles, and the meat. But once these parts are finished, you can assemble a pie in pretty much no time at all.

This recipe is scaled down to make two large portions, but you should know that this makes a great dish for a crowd. Judge the garnishes by eye and heat as many beans as you want to eat. For a meatless version, replace the beef with sautéed zucchini and corn, or just season the cooked beans with the red chile and let it go at that.

By the way, "chile" refers to the red chile sauce. Add the meat, and you have "chili," the dish.

1. Break the tops (stem end) off the chiles, tear them open, and shake out the seeds and discard. Put the chiles in a pot, cover with water, and bring to a boil. Cover and simmer for 20 minutes, then turn off the heat and let them stand another 10 minutes. Drain, then purée the chiles with 1½ cups fresh water for at least 1 minute. Pass this through a strainer, press out all the liquid you can, and discard the debris. Season with ½ teaspoon salt. Taste the chile and, if it seems a little harsh, add a few drops of vinegar to soften it.

2. Heat the oil in a skillet and crumble in the meat. Cook over medium-low heat (especially if it's grass-fed beef or bison, which tend to be lean) until the meat is just cooked. Season with salt. Pour in the chile (but not so much that it's soupy) and taste. Add more salt if needed. Cook over low heat while you warm up the beans and prepare the fresh toppings.

3. Place the beans in a shallow, wide bowl. Add the Fritos or tortilla chips, then spoon over as much chili as you want, saving the rest for another meal. Scatter a little cheese over the top and then heap the lettuce, tomato, cilantro, and onion or scallions over all.

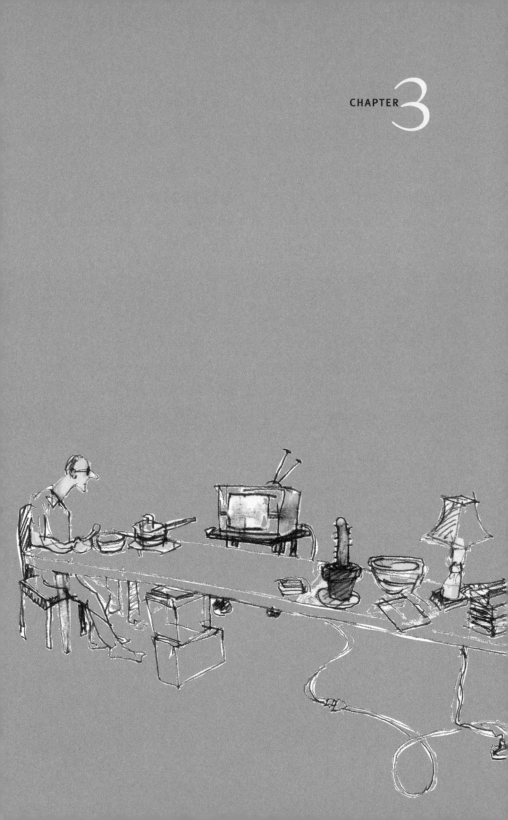

CHAPTER 3

Foods for Me and Me Alone

"I cook a pot of white jasmine rice, then I scramble two eggs
with salt and pepper. I stir the eggs into the hot rice, and then
add a dollop of full fat Brown Cow yogurt with more salt. It's
weird but it's comforting. I read while I'm eating and my dog
curls up at my feet. This is a totally personal food—not one I'd
share with anyone."

—Blake Spalding, *Chef of Hell's Backbone Grill*

GREG O'BYRNE, WHO RUNS THE SANTA FE WINE AND CHILE FIESTA, is not embarrassed to admit that he spoils himself on nights when he's home alone. He doesn't cook the mac and cheese he usually

makes for his kids, but opens a bottle of wine, "maybe not a Grand Cru Burgundy, but a good bottle," he says, and he fixes himself a thick steak *au poivre*. He's likely to make his own *pommes frites*, too.

More frequently, though, foods intended for solo consumption tend to be modest, sometimes crude, and often downright bizarre. They're very personal foods, that special category of edibles that are tailored by oneself for oneself, and they are not easily shared. They're the foods that work for one individual in a deep and maybe even psychological way. Personal foods are likely to be those that simply gratify. They might have nourished us as children and now they feed us as adults, regardless of their content, because our body knows and remembers them.

Take Dru Sherrod, for example, a tall, elegant man with whom we've enjoyed many well-cooked meals and fine bottles of wine. Only the faintest trace of his Texas accent remains. Here was his response when we asked him what he eats when his partner, Arden, is out of town.

"Back in Dallas," Dru says, sliding into his accent, "my mother used to serve me fried Spam with grape jelly. Well, after eschewing it for forty years, I'm beginning to find it a great comfort again. I throw slabs of Spam in a skillet. Thick units. No oil or butter or anything. Fry it on both sides. Slice some tomatoes. Spoon out cottage cheese. It's salty, porky, strong, greasy, and delicious. A perfect meal." And now he's talking Texan.

Or consider Robert Brittan, a journeyman winemaker. We're driving one morning over the winding roads of the coast range near Napa Valley, and he's waving his arms madly as he answers our question. Fortunately he's not the one behind the wheel.

"Fritos!" he cries. "Take chili-cheese-flavored Fritos, microwave them with grated cheese. Fantastic! Or, have them with chopped green tomatoes. *Chopped*, not sliced. Slicing is overrated—it implies care. You can chop these tomatoes with a dull knife—just beat 'em up.

This is fantastic when you first eat it. It's only after you've eaten too much that you realize Fritos are nasty and ugly. The good thing is you can drink lousy beer with them. Doesn't matter. Anyway, it's about what you've got."

It's hard to see this wildly gesticulating Frito maniac as the same man who meticulously crafts exquisite Pinots and Syrahs, but that's the thing about eat-alone food: it's not consistent with those sides of ourselves that the world, including close friends, sees.

"It's about experimentation," says Robert, not yet finished with the subject. "Do you know, you can boil a hot dog in cheap beer or wine? Once I got this Hebrew National Hot Dog and cooked it in Riesling. Any Riesling will do." But other experiments fail. "Chocolate chip ice cream in root beer makes an okay float. But beer in a milk shake? I can tell you it's a horrible, horrible thing."

HERE ARE SOME OF THE ODD THINGS THAT PEOPLE CONFESS TO EATING

Saltines crumbled in milk

Oyster crackers or matzo in coffee

Life Cereal dredged with Coffee-Mate, the original formula only, none of that low-fat or flavored junk

Cream of Wheat made with lumps

Dried cereal with broken butter cookies, drowned in milk

Wonder Bread, flattened, covered with butter and sugar, then frozen briefly, so it becomes a kind of sugar cookie

Cake batter (especially chocolate) and raw cookie dough (especially chocolate chip)

Frozen pound cake shaved into thin pieces and eaten cold

Leftover spaghetti that's stuck together, fried with Swiss cheese

A baked potato covered with cottage cheese and a smashed up hard-boiled egg

People who don't normally put a lot of stock into recipes can be extremely precise about their personal foods, such as how milk should look when poured over hot cereal ("It should just puddle around the edges, no more, or it will cool down the cereal and thin it out"), or the kind of bread used for a sandwich ("It *must* be white bread, like Wonder Bread, not a sturdier variety like Pepperidge Farms"), or the potato chips used to scoop up cottage cheese ("*Only* use Ruffles"), or how long eggs must be cooked ("Six minutes, not five or seven, but six").

However strange, these foods do accomplish the work of getting a body fed.

When we began our survey with men, we secretly took pleasure in uncovering those nasty true confessions, the crude stuff, the so-called recipes that make any decent eater cringe—in short, the strange foods of the solitary eater. We got them from both men and women. Things—we can't really call them dishes—like bread soaked in margarita mix, or sardine oil poured over cottage cheese. *Who* would do this, you may ask? Well, relatively normal people, it turns out. Perhaps even your own friends.

Cliff Wright, the author of many good cookbooks and one of the best cooks we know, has this tactic for feeding himself. "Sometimes when I'm on a recipe-testing roll, I end up with six Tupperware containers filled with leftover god-knows-what. I'll take them all, dump them in a bowl of pasta, and start tossing. If the taste isn't quite right, I add one or all of the following: fried pancetta, butter, cream, olive oil, prosciutto, egg, or cheese."

I especially like the flourish of "one or all" of those fatty additions, and nothing in between, like butter and cheese. Of course, Cliff has a pretty good idea of what he's doing, so he's likely to end up with something that's more than merely edible despite his slapdash approach. (Not always slapdash, Cliff has been known to use an otherwise spacious Sunday afternoon intended for reading to whip up a batch of crepinettes, a sausage-like affair that involves three kinds of meat, vegetables, and caulfat—and these just for himself.)

Personal foods may not be shareable, but that doesn't mean that they aren't good to eat or aren't enjoyed by more than just one or two odd souls. More than a few of our respondents mentioned stirring oyster crackers, saltines, matzo, or some other crumbly dry thing into cups of tea, coffee, milk, and cocoa. In *Cheri* and *The Last of Cheri*, Colette writes about just this sort of thing, but in a way that makes you want to go right into the kitchen and try it for yourself— or at least recast the description of your own personal concoction in a more poetic way.

> Take a small soup tureen—the individual soup tureen you would use for a *soupe gratinée*, or a sturdy bowl in fireproof china. Pour in your milky coffee, prepared and sugared according to taste. Cut some hearty slices of bread—use household bread, refined white will not do—butter them lavishly and lay them on the coffee, ensuring that they are not submerged. Then all you have to do is place the whole thing in the oven and leave it there until your breakfast is browned and crusty, with fat buttery bubbles sizzling here and there on the surface.

Finally, Colette advises, "Before breaking your raft of roasted bread, sprinkle on some salt." Even a small trace of salt counteracts the sugar and makes everything sharp and bright.

I copied this passage from a book in someone else's library over twenty years ago because it spoke to me, but I never thought to write down the translator, who remains a mystery still. In the attempt to find this translation, I started reading various others. A less lavish version turned the same breakfast into something so prosaic that I read through practically the whole paragraph before recognizing the raft-crusted bowl of coffee. Perhaps the tender attention to detail in the first translation is what turned a somewhat rough and personal dish into nothing less than a morning sacrament. If so, with the right words, oyster crackers in coffee might be equally sacramental.

Oyster crackers in coffee, yes, but perhaps our woman in the kitchen uses a cup with an especially wide mouth and enough cream to turn the black filtered coffee the color of ivory. I wonder if the oyster crackers cover the surface, so that they just touch one another, or not. Does she take a sip of coffee with a cracker from a spoon? Is the cracker soft below and crisp on top? As she goes along, does she add more crackers? One by one or by the handful?

I've never had coffee with oyster crackers so I don't know the nature of its particular charms, but surely there would be those minute particulars that say *why* coffee and *why* oyster crackers and not some other kind, the very details that make personal foods so important.

Largely, though, personal foods are stunningly strange. The following examples are offered for your amusement only, as these aren't things we could make into recipes, and we don't think you should either.

1. MUSTARD SANDWICH WITH REWORKED COFFEE: "Use Yellow Heinz Mustard. Slather the mustard on a flour tortilla and eat accompanied with reworked coffee, which means add a few new grounds to the top of a paper filter of morning coffee and pour in boiling water."

2. POTATO-SESAME BREAD WITH TEQUILA MIX: "Toss an old loaf of potato-sesame bread on a wood-burning stove. Tear into hunks and eat with tequila mix right out of the plastic bottle."

3. ORGANIC GOO GOO: "Get Green Giant small whole peas and one package of any Green Giant rice mix—Asian, Mexican, and so forth. Make a small cut in the top to prevent an explosion, and microwave them in their own microwavable pouches. During the six or so minutes they're cooking, look in the spice closet and find some less-than-a-year-old spice, a young spice. Any spice will do. Cut open the two hot pouches with a knife and pour on a plate with the rice on the bottom, the peas on the top. Sprinkle with spice. This fits right into the Asian diet pyramid. It's a good dish if you don't have a maid or a dishwasher, since it uses only a fork, a knife, and a plate."

4. LEFTOVER SPAGHETTI SANDWICH: Usually in cooking, the whole is more than the sum of its parts. Here, it is less. The day after a big spaghetti feed, a friend—who is most of the time a good and lusty kind of cook—uses the leftovers to make spaghetti sandwiches.

"I rewarm the garlic bread in the toaster and the tomato sauce and the pasta in a pan, then make a sandwich adding whatever soggy salad kind of thing I have left over, usually tomato, onion, and translucent lettuce."

5. FARM WORKERS' FOOD: A farmer in Texas talks about how his workers cook when they're out in the country on an isolated farm, cooking and coping for themselves. Try to hear the slow drawl, the chili-thick accent, and a liberal sprinkling of expletives. Although it was winter when Larry Butler reported to us, I think the word "cold" means raw.

"They take sardines, cold Romas, cold onions, chop and mix, and put it on a hot corn tortilla. Or they start with some Top Ramen noodles, scramble up an egg and put it in the pot along with a can of green English peas. They also boil pork rinds until they're disgusting and terrible looking and throw them, with fried onions, into scrambled eggs, then put it all in a hot tortilla. And they eat this stuff like it's good!"

In self-defense, Larry, who's a vegetarian, retreats to his out-door kitchen. "Up front I sauté wheat berries with garlic in olive oil on high heat. Wheat berries give you something to chew on. I put garlic in all foods. Chop turnips, onions, carrots, and beets and add to the sauté, then add cold tomatoes if I have them. About the time it's going to catch fire and explode, I put in tomato juice and nutritional yeast—the yeast gives body, flavor, and B vitamins—add more water, then cook for 30 minutes."

Meanwhile, back on their urban farm in East Austin, Larry's wife, Carol Ann Sayle, reports that she is likely to be having "a glass of wine with Seinfeld, to be followed later by some granola with raw goat milk" for her solo dinner.

I suspect that none of these meals are interchangeable even though all the parties know each other well and two are even married to each other. Each is right only for the one who cooked it.

Why, and for whom, you might ask, do people produce food magazines and cookbooks, host cooking shows and culinary tours, and indulge in all the other culinary hoopla? Behind closed doors it's a free-for-all out there, even for otherwise sophisticated eaters. But it does get better. And some personal foods do make sense, in a way. A doctor friend volunteered that he often does something thoughtless, like indulging his serious sweet tooth with cookies and ice cream. And then he added, without our having even mentioned the idea of personal foods, that he had a favorite unshareable dessert, a small bowl of Grape-Nuts with vanilla ice cream.

Because personal foods are just that, *personal*, there are no recipes in this chapter. But we do think that Grape-Nuts with vanilla ice cream would be almost universally enjoyed. In fact, we learned recently, this is actually a popular ice cream flavor in Canada.

Getting the Body Fed
with Rough and Ready Foods

"When I'm cooking for myself, it happens like an urge. That is, it probably isn't a regular mealtime. I first notice that I'm hungry and then have a vision of something that's in the fridge or the pantry. Then I dream up a recipe for it."

—Moky McKelvey, *musician and graphic designer*

ALTHOUGH I WAS HEADING OUT THE DOOR, I had to take a quick kitchen detour and peek in the oven to see what smelled so good. Inside were seven big potatoes baking away. They were almost adorable, the way they were all lined up in a row. But it did seem like a lot of potatoes.

"It saves on propane and, besides, there are lots of things I can do with baked potatoes," Patrick explained. Clearly, he's an example of one who doesn't mind eating the same thing over and over again.

How *do* men feed themselves when they're home alone?

In different ways, of course. A neighbor tells us that he doesn't mind taking two hours to cook his dinner when he's alone. (His wife, on the other hand, turns to frozen macaroni and cheese, delighted not to think about cooking for a change.) Other men go out to eat on a regular basis. And some happily make do with something they can eat off of for days, like a pot of chili, a ham—or potatoes.

Men also eat things their wives don't care for, like greasy sausages, brains, or eggs fried in a lake of bacon grease, the hot fat spooned over the yolks. Some dishes are rustled up out of what's around the fridge and in the cupboard, rustic meals that could be made better, but left unimproved, provide a decent feeding. Both members of one couple we spoke with make their meals entirely out of what they can buy in liquor stores—jerky, trail mix, pretzels, Ritz crackers with peanut butter—which they dine on whether together or alone. While having a liquor store as one's main food source doesn't sound quite right, there is an argument for a dinner consisting of a Scotch and a bowl of peanuts. There are days when that's a perfect meal—

days when lunch lasted too late or one was stuck in town at a meeting, days when one wants a little soothing sustenance when it's all over, but not much. Whatever the approach, here are some of the simpler dishes made mostly by men, though not entirely, on their own. In case you're wondering why there's not a lot of meat here, it's because meat looms larger in the next chapter. This is the "healthy eating" part of men cooking for themselves.

Something both men and women frequently express enthusiasm for is the leftover. With leftovers one can cobble pieces of former meals into new ones without investing a lot of time in the process. In addition, eating leftovers has ecological implications, which we discovered through an article that came over the Internet called *Eat*

Leftovers, Save the World. Good title, big message. It came from the UK but no doubt applies to the US as well. It seems that discarded food accounts for a fifth of the United Kingdom's carbon emissions, and decomposing food releases that most potent of greenhouse gasses, methane. The 6.7 million tons each year of so-called garbage—we say "so-called" because much of that food is still edible when disposed, apparently—creates an even bigger problem than packaging waste, and it represents a third of all food purchased. Amazing! (Martin Hickman, *London Independent*, November 2, 2007)

Knowing this should make us want to eat our leftovers. Or, if we don't like leftovers, it might encourage us to cook less in the first place. And failing that, we might want to compost those foods we don't eat. Patrick, a reluctant composter who laughed at my piles of vegetable peelings rotting in the backyard until he read this article, now brings home buckets of scraps from his studio to add to those very heaps that will eventually nourish the garden.

"It's one small step for mankind," Patrick announces as he adds his contribution to the compost pile.

Despite the considerable advantages to eating leftovers, we discovered that there are those who openly detest leftover food, those who wouldn't dream of taking home a partially eaten dinner from a restaurant or reheating food left from another meal. But mostly we love the foods that remain, depend on leftovers, seek them out, and are grateful when we find them. And for reasons other than ease and convenience.

Peach farmer and writer Mas Masamoto, for example, turns to leftovers when he's alone because, he says, "I immediately miss my wife, and leftovers are a way of reliving a meal. I have often wondered how someone eats after a spouse or partner dies. Reliving a meal can be both sad and yet memorable. Besides, leftovers are usually not that bad."

For less contemplative men, leftovers are favorites because all you have to do is reheat them, if that. There are some leftovers that started out hot but have been known to go down cold, like frittatas or roast chicken. Even spaghetti. Then there are those that actually develop flavor as they sit, like stews and soups. One remaindered food that works well for some is polenta.

Patrick describes his joy at encountering a bowl of leftover polenta and sliding it into a pan of hot olive oil where it sputters and hisses before finally falling apart. It really was a little too wet for frying, but no one else would see how messy the final dish would look. Besides, frying has its own special appeal. After five minutes Patrick manages to turn over what is now a virtual mess of cornmeal mush. Some of it sticks to the pan, but these crispy bits get scraped up and folded into the whole.

"The crisp parts are the good parts, after all," he explains, "but it does look a bit plain and jumbled." To remedy the situation, he slices a ball of fresh mozzarella and stews it over the polenta. "But," he adds helpfully, "if you don't have mozzarella, it would work just as well with Gorgonzola or some leftover crumbs of another blue cheese. Or any cheese, really."

"I had a lid, but it was too small, so I propped it up against the spatula, which was resting in the pan." Patrick was cooking at his studio, not at home, which isn't perfectly equipped with matching lids and pans. "It covered everything just enough to melt the cheese. I served it up. Black pepper and red pepper flakes went on top. And when I saw that more of that good crusty stuff was stuck to the pan, I just scraped it out and added it to the plate."

Messy or not, don't you know this would be good? I wished I had been there. If I had, I would have chopped a little fresh thyme for the polenta, made a salad, and brought out those leftover poached pears that Patrick had apparently overlooked. But that's what happens when another person joins in. What was a perfectly good single-plate, one-pan dinner for a solitary diner suddenly becomes a full-fledged multidish meal for two.

Polenta works for another Arkansan also named Patrick. Because he likes to cook and doesn't mind spending a little time in front of the stove, it's not surprising that this was easy to make into a shareable recipe. Patrick McKelvey seasons his freshly cooked polenta with a pinch of marjoram, then pours it onto a lightly oiled plate. "While it sets up, I slowly sauté a mashed garlic clove and a thinly sliced onion until soft. I wilt a handful of greens in the onion mixture, chop a couple of slices of prosciutto and toss them in for the last few minutes. Then I let it catch its breath. I pour all of this over the polenta, which I've now sliced up, and grate some Parmesan over that. Pour a glass of red wine and that'll do."

By the way, **polenta** is not hard to make from scratch, and you absolutely do not have to stir it for an hour—or even for a half-hour—unless, of course, you want to. You also don't have to let it set, although that takes only a few minutes. You can spoon it warm and soft onto a plate and pile the greens on top.

The Galisteo Inn, which is practically next door to us, had polenta with a vegetable ragout on the menu one night. It looked especially tempting to a robust, dreadlock-sporting African American potter named Sam Harvey, and a discussion about its possibilities ensued. Sam liked the sound of the dish because it reminded him of what he cooks for himself.

"When I eat alone, which is most of the time," Sam said, "I put on grits and after they've cooked for ten or fifteen minutes, I throw in some vegetables and fresh garlic. I use frozen veggies out of the bag. Peas are good, and so is corn, but any vegetable will do. Then I finish with some grated Parmesan. I have this for breakfast and for lunch. But for dinner I throw the frozen veggies in a skillet with olive oil, add water, sardines from a can or that other fish with a rich taste—anchovies!—maybe cubes of tofu or chunks of whatever protein is on sale. And I make a salad with olive oil and lemon juice for a dressing."

I was impressed that Sam made the dressing for his salad. Finally, here was someone who wasn't seduced by the false promises of bottled dressings built on dull oils, xantham gums, and corn syrup. But as a vegetable lover, I was somewhat dismayed by all those frozen veggies. But Sam spoke up for them as others have. "Frozen vegetables are terribly underrated. There are so many kinds and they don't go bad! You can break off just what you want to use and return the rest to the freezer without worry."

In the end, Sam ordered the salmon because, after all, grits and vegetables are what he cooks every day, and I had the polenta. And in the spirit of compromise, I came up with a dish for Sam that uses both fresh and frozen vegetables over polenta—corn on corn with scallions and shrimp, which might work for someone willing to cook something but not everything. In other words, polenta with corn and scallions plus sautéed shrimp is a partial slam-dunk approach.

A number of men like to modify canned
soup. I am a fan of canned lentil soup simply
modified, and I've also eaten my share of Amy's
organic tomato soup with additions of avocado,
lime juice, sour cream, and other goodies. You
can improve a lot of canned or boxed soups using
this method. Or expand upon them, I should say,
for you should start with a decent soup to begin
with and then make it better.

Patrick of the **polenta smothered with braised greens** recom-
mends doctoring up chicken noodle soup by mashing a clove of garlic,
then "carelessly chopping five or six kalamata olives until the stones
escape." Next, he sautés these in a tablespoon or so of good olive
oil, "until they begin to be noticed," and finally dumps them in the
chicken noodle soup and brings it to a simmer. "Let it simmer until
it's all bubbly, then turn off the heat for a few minutes rest. Crumble
up soda crackers in a bowl and pour the hot soup over that. Yum!"

An even simpler way to enhance a soup, especially a bean soup,
invariably involves such basic ingredients as a capful of extra-virgin
olive oil, a few parsley sprigs (or another herb) chopped with some
garlic, freshly ground pepper, and shavings of Parmesan cheese. Toast is
also good served on the side or broken up and added to the soup.

Toast, in fact, has been known to comprise the main part of the
dinner menu for more than one solitary eater. This particularly simple
means to a meal came from a Spanish chef and guitar player we met
in Madrid. His answer to our question? "Grill sliced bread with butter
on both sides in a skillet. Serve it with marmalade."

That's it! Not much of a meal, perhaps, but satisfying, especially
if you need to be nourished after feeding others. Being a chef, he'd

probably already tasted a lot of food while at work, and he just might have wanted to sit down to something that wasn't on the menu, wasn't a sample or a leftover, and wasn't a plate shared with others. Crisp, buttered pan toast and marmalade would do the trick. No artifice involved, no chance of failure, just a good, honest bite to eat.

Another man, not a chef, also turned to toast when batching it. He calls his recipe "Meat and Toast." We were a little wary of it, but then, it wasn't the only time we had heard of pairing bacon with peanut butter. Here's what he says to do:

"Nuke four pieces of peppered bacon wrapped in a paper towel until crisp but still juicy, about 3 minutes in the average microwave. Meanwhile, toast a slice of whatever bread you favor until brown and good smelling, then slather it with crunchy peanut butter. Chew a bit of bacon, take a bite of toast, have a slurp of coffee. Ahhhhh."

A panini machine has provided Patrick with an endless parade of good things to eat that are shelved between festive slices of grilled bread. Never inclined to make a regular sandwich, Patrick has taken to his panini machine with gusto. "Panini are warm and so much more satisfying to eat on a cold day than cold sandwiches," he explains. "Plus you can make two kinds at once, and you can slice them and serve them as appetizers." And you can forever improvise with the fillings. His **panini with mustard greens and roasted peppers** has become a house classic, along with one made of grilled cheese and roasted green chile. When we made the bartender's grilled flank steak stuffed with mushrooms and more, we had a lot of the mushroom filling left over, as well as some Gruyère cheese. "All those fillings went into panini the next day and a day or two after that, and it was so good that now I make a version from scratch," says Patrick.

A fried egg sandwich is another toast-based meal that has its avid supporters. I myself am a huge fan of fried egg sandwiches—those crisp slices of wholesome toast, a really fresh egg from the farmers market, lots of pepper, and good butter. Owen Rubin told me about the fried egg sandwich he makes when his wife, Dianne, is away. He has a great twist on this classic: he fries, rather than toasts, his bread, but only on one side. I saw how this worked when he made one for my breakfast—the crunchy buttery side goes in toward the egg, and the soft and greaseless sides are the ones you hold so your fingers don't end up all greasy. Owen topped his with pro-sciutto and cheese, but of course, fried egg sandwiches can be less—or more—complicated. A recent favorite, for example, puts a fluffy cheese omelet with bacon and smoked chile between sliced, but not toasted, rosemary focaccia.

Another man, one in the food-importing business, also turns to toast, only his is covered with tomato sauce. "This is a spiceless recipe," he declares. "You must *not* go near a spice rack. I mean *no* spice. Just toast an English muffin, pour a ton of Prego mushroom ragu over it, grate some cheese over the whole thing, and bake it in a toaster oven."

This isn't that far away from tomatoes on toast, a woman's favorite. The ragu makes for a somewhat lustier topping, or try our version of an **English muffin with (spiceless) ragu and sharp cheddar.** It happily recalls that nostalgic pairing of canned tomato soup and cheese sandwiches, only it's better, even without spice.

We've known farmers who, exhausted at the end of a long market day, will pick up a pizza for dinner. But Ed May, another farmer we used to know before he gave up farming in New Mexico and moved to Hawaii to tend a macadamia nut orchard, used to grow between twenty and thirty varieties of potatoes. Ed once hosted a potato-tasting party in which boiled potatoes were mindfully tasted, notes dutifully taken, and then washed down with as many varieties of vodka as there were tubers. That was fun and informative, but on more everyday occasions, Ed claimed to satisfy his solo cravings by covering toast not with potatoes, but with ratatouille, or his version of it.

He prefaced his bachelor supper, saying, "I've gotten so lazy," and then went on to describe making his ratatouille from scratch with roasted peppers, onion, garlic, eggplant, zucchini, and, finally, tomatoes. (Remember, not only did Ed start with raw materials in the kitchen, he actually grew them as well.) After making his stew, he pan-toasted bread with butter, oregano, basil, and thyme, then poured the ratatouille over the toast, still in its skillet, and melted some cheese on top of that, covering the whole thing with a lid. Not exactly your classic ratatouille, but good enough by far.

On other days when Ed was no doubt unspeakably lazy, he would dig up some of his fingerling potatoes, sprinkle New Mexican red chile over them, and put them in a pan with butter, garlic, and a bit of onion. "Then I roast the whole thing in the oven and put Parmesan on top when the potatoes are done."

This is good. Even our simpler version is very good. So good that it's hard to eat just twenty-five golden roasted potato wedges dusted in smoldering red chile.

In contrast to Ed and his homegrown farmer's cooking, there's James Holmes, a Quaker cowboy artist and master of gutsy male cooking with an eye on the fat. Take, for example, his dish for chili con carne, which he makes when his wife is out playing in her country band. He swears it takes thirty minutes from start to finish.

"Buy ground sirloin. It's low in fat," he instructs. "Throw it in the pot without any oil, but add a little beer. Brown the meat and add three cans of pinto beans with jalapeños. Or you can substitute one can of Ranch Style black beans. Don't drain them; use them right out of the can. Throw in cinnamon and brown sugar and get it all cooking for twenty minutes. Put in some *masa harina*, 6 or 7 cloves of garlic, then add chopped cilantro and cook for one or two more minutes."

This would be rather garlicky, we imagine, which is fine if it's just you and your horse. But this isn't true for James's **potatoes with green chile**, a classic combination in these parts. "Steam cubed potatoes or boil them in chicken broth and skip the butter. Mash them

BEANS

BEER

with crushed garlic. Add roasted green chile and a bump of cumin," he says. "And plan on beer for your beverage."

The same roasted green chile also goes into James's range gazpacho. "Take onion, tomato, cilantro, bell pepper, carrot, and more green chile, chunk it up in some V-juice, add lots of black pepper, and let it sit in the refrigerator. You've never had a gazpacho like this, but it's not bad for range cooking," James says.

Staying with the Southwest theme, a burrito is another basic food that does a good job of filling up that hollow leg. If you have beans, tortillas, cheese, and eggs, and, of course, some salsa or some good red chili, you can feed yourself all week, maybe even forever, on burritos. Breakfast or supper, they can be the same or they can differ. Actor John Flax has his own version of the burrito.

"I get a tortilla and put some steamed spinach in there with a chopped-up baked potato, yellow cheese, and hot sauce out of a bottle. Wrap it up in tinfoil and bake it in a toaster oven. Then peel back the foil, add more sauce, and eat."

Scrambled eggs are also good with the potatoes and spinach, or alone, and an eggy **breakfast burrito** is one you can eat day or night.

Do men eat salads when they're on their own? One describes what he eats as pretty basic stuff, and that includes salads. "Whatever's in the refrigerator," he says, "but no exotic lettuces. I find them too bitter. Carrots, regular lettuce, throw whatever in and put on a little olive oil. Done. Finished."

A wine and architectural enthusiast says that if it's just him alone he eats "pretty healthy." That is, he makes a salad "with greens and stuff, including arugula." But the three eat-alone meals he described—steak sandwiches with asparagus, frijoles with salsa fresca, and *chilaquiles,* sound nothing like salad even if they do sound good. As for their being pretty healthy, you can decide.

The idea of cooking a lot of asparagus and drawing from it at will is a good one. Just simmer it in salted water until it's tender, let it drain on a clean towel, and refrigerate. Dress it just before you eat it so it doesn't go gray on you. It's simple and straightforward, and you can do that with lots of vegetables—beets, green beans, and artichokes, too.

Although this is mostly a man's chapter, Amelia Saltsman also turns to a platter of roasted asparagus to eat off of over a few days, only hers is a bit more done up. "I roast two big bunches of the first thick asparagus from the farmers market with a bit of olive oil, Maldon sea salt, and black pepper. I boil up three Aurcana eggs (the blue ones), and make a whole-grain mustard vinaigrette. I crumble the eggs over the asparagus, pour the vinaigrette over all, and scatter some toasted stale, torn bread on that and, of course, a little more crunchy salt. I pick up the spears one by one. No utensils required other than a soup spoon to scoop up any bits of egg and dressing at the end. I eat half the first day, warm, most of the rest cold the next day for lunch, and the last bit as a snack late in the day." We highly recommend this dish.

Our male solo eater enjoyed his asparagus to eat all week with the tri-tip that he grills and uses for steak sandwiches. The tri-tip is mostly known as a California cut that's mainly featured in Santa Maria barbecue, but it is gradually becoming better known outside of the area. (I just spied a tri-tip tortilla wrap in Trader Joe's, so you know it's getting out there.) Our local rancher who sells grass-fed beef at the farmers market knew right away what it was and even had one on hand. "But you have to cut it thin," he warned. And you really do. It's a tough one.

"You might prefer a grilled flank steak," commented a friend, surprised that anyone would recommend a tri-tip, although marinating does help.

Regardless, the instructions are, "Put good olive oil on bread and oregano on the thinly sliced meat. Add lettuce and tomato, and serve it with the asparagus." And that's his sandwich.

For his *frijoles,* or **pretty plain** pinto beans, he soaks pinto beans, "a dried bag of them," cooks them with salt pork and lard, and then eats them with tortillas. "I make a meal of this with salsa out of a bottle. But in the summer, I make a **salsa fresca** out of tomatoes and onion, chopped fine, and celery for texture. Sometimes I throw in corn. And I add cilantro, and vinegar, and oil." We suspect this might be as close to salad as we're going to get.

His chilaquiles is a good, messy dish and is another practical approach that blends time at the stove with chips from a bag. "Shuck tomatillos and boil them in chicken broth with garlic and jalapeño peppers," his recipe begins. "The key is the peppers. Some are a lot hotter than others, so you need to taste them. Sometimes it takes three peppers, other times just one. In any case, throw it all in a blender and give it short, jerky jolts until you have the consistency you want. You can put this in a jar and keep it in the fridge. Once you've got a supply of sauce, you take tortilla chips, put them in a skillet and pour the sauce on top. Put a couple of fried eggs on top of that and drizzle over Mexican crema." And there you have it.

This may sound funky, and it is. But it's also really good. If you're lucky enough to find a good fresh tomatillo salsa made by some enterprising local cook, then it's a matter of very few minutes before you're sitting down to a delicious dinner, or breakfast, for that matter. If not, make your own. It's easy and it's worth it.

Let us introduce the one-ingredient driven cook, Dan Welch, who has been, among other things, a traveling pizza maker, an artist, and a Zen monk with an appetite for all foods hot and fiery. Dan has been cooking with a beginner's mind for more than thirty years. When you eat with Dan, you have to ignore the mess he makes in the kitchen, overlook the excessive amounts of dripping fat from bacon and olive oil, deal with the heat, and just dig in without reserve. It's always worth it.

As a lone eater, Dan has never gotten sloppy and skipped an opportunity to make food, especially **tapenade**, which is, in effect, his most basic ingredient, the very base, in fact, of his personal food pyramid. He's made children cry and adults wither with this condiment, which has far more chile flakes than any authentic version. There's a certain theme to Dan's food. In fact, it's all variations on a theme, but what a theme! There's always tapenade, chile, pork in some form (unless he's behaving like a vegetarian), tongue-searing salsas, and some pungent goat cheese, Gorgonzola, or gooey melting cheese. These ingredients are variously folded into tortillas, sandwiched between slices of toasted levain bread, or tossed with hot strands of spaghetti. These dishes come from an era when Dan was taking a break from monastic life. At that time, poison eggs were a big part of his diet.

"I get poisoned rain or shine, company or no," he used to say. And he still gets poisoned, but not every day.

Here's an easy version of the recipe.

"I make two poach-fried eggs, which means you start frying them in olive oil, then add a tablespoon of water, cover the pan, and steam until the yolks are as firm as you like them to be. Then I fold

them in a warm flour tortilla with tapenade, Muenster cheese, avocado, salsa fresca, bacon, sausage, prosciutto, steak, or whatever meat is left-over from another time." Or, you can skip the meat. The only part you need is the recipe for tapenade, which, in Dan's words, goes like this: "Combine in descending order of quantity, chopped kalamata olives, capers, anchovies, olive oil, lemon juice, garlic, and red chile flakes."

The **open-faced melted cheese sandwich** that Dan consumes on a regular basis is also made with tapenade. It's easy and, not surprisingly, predictable.

"First melt cheese (Muenster, again, is named) on levain bread in a toaster oven, top it with tapenade, then add cucumber, avocado, or tomato. Wash it down with a Dos Equis, then take a nap."

Chipotle chile is another one of Dan's basic food groups. He packs a vial of it at all times to wake up any bland café food he might encounter on the road, and he uses it to make an addictive mayonnaise. His fundamental food choices may seem narrow, but they are good building blocks for the solo eater who wants fire and fat.

When I asked the "What do you eat?" question in a workshop I was giving at Tassajara Zen Mountain Center, Marty, who had said almost nothing during the entire class, quickly volunteered for this one. He had it all worked out.

"When alone, I eat standing up next to the sink," he started off saying, describing what you might think of as typical man-alone behavior. Then he went into the details.

"I pick the oldest and fastest foods to prepare, or what my wife doesn't want," he continues. The oldest food? The food that needs most to be eaten? This we hadn't heard before, except from our teacher, Suzuki-roshi, who, when he had the occasion to shop for his own food after first coming to America, also used to choose the oldest, saddest vegetables. Someone had to eat them. His father, also a Zen priest, was known to pluck vegetables discarded by farmers out of the stream and then cook them. This approach, both tender and fierce, is not one that's often talked about. In Marty's case, it may have been about sympathy for the oldest vegetables, but it was also about frugality.

"I'm genetically frugal," he explained. "For example, we had some sliced Velveeta cheese around for a long time. I bought it, lots of it, by mistake for a big party we were having. I couldn't throw it away, so I ended up making a lot of toasted cheese sandwiches over a period of many months.

"First I get some bread out of the freezer. Multigrain is best for long-term freezing," Marty explains, saying he's had quite a bit of experience freezing bread.

"Second, I toast the bread," he continues. I assume he adds the cheese about now.

"Third, I find those things that have been there for months, like pepper jelly. The correct amount is important. Too little and it's too bland, too much and it's too much."

I suspect that a lot of us have ancient opened jars of pepper jellies and chutneys and other condiments hidden, forgotten about, neglected, and ignored that we'd do well to use up. And this is not a bad combo. In fact a grilled cheese and pepper jelly sandwich can be very good indeed. I recall my grandmother sitting down to a quiet morning bite of toasted rye bread with Cheddar and jam or marmalade. For her, it wouldn't have been pepper jelly, but the salty-sweet twist of the rye, cheese, and jam is what makes such combinations appealing. Add chile or vinegar, and they're even more interesting.

"While I'm chewing," Marty continues, "I go to the pantry and look around for cookies. If it's a really bad day and there aren't any, I get another piece of bread and make toast and jelly. And I drink V-8 juice. It's my healthy compensation."

And not a word about eating over the sink. Marty is, it turns out, a pacer.

In contrast to all this cooking, there's Charlie Johnston, a retired banker from Arkansas, who's had one too many hip replacements. He isn't too keen on cooking. Patrick has even sent him boxes of soup in the mail, and his friends who are geographically closer try to help out in the kitchen as well.

"Cooking messes up the kitchen too much," Charlie says. "Cooking is a stand-up sport. I can think about breakfast, but cooking is a pain in the ass. No wonder women rebelled."

POLENTA

Polenta is one of those fundamental foods on which you can build entire meals. Many say that 1 cup of polenta cooked in a quart of water will serve four, but it's more likely to feed a hungry man just once or twice.

1 cup polenta

salt

butter or grated cheese

Bring 4 cups of water to a boil. Gradually stir in the polenta in a slow, steady stream, then add 1 teaspoon of salt. Lower the heat to medium and cook, still stirring, until the polenta has absorbed enough water to make a more or less even mass. Then, lower the heat still more, almost as low as it will go. At this point you can leave it pretty much alone, stirring it just every now and then to make sure it isn't sticking. It needs 30 minutes to really be cooked, but the longer it cooks after that, the fuller the flavor will be. Once done, taste for salt and add more if needed. Leave as is, or add butter or freshly grated Parmigiano-Reggiano cheese. Odds and ends of cheese are good too, such as fontina, mozzarella, and crumbs of Gorgonzola or other blues.

Soft Polenta. At this point you can pour the soft polenta onto your plate and add whatever else you're having with it—sautéed mushrooms (page 164), braised greens, or blue cheese sauce (page 196).

Firm Polenta. For discrete pieces, pour the warm polenta into a bowl lightly brushed with olive oil, let it stand while you cook your topping, then turn it out. Now you can slice it and put wedges of polenta on the plate, or you can fry the pieces in olive oil or butter before serving.

Leftover polenta will already be firm when you take it from the refrigerator. Slice it, then brown it in butter or olive oil. If you like it better soft, put it in a saucepan, add water to thin it out, whisk to make it smooth, and reheat. (Polenta, by the way, makes a warming breakfast cereal: flavor soft polenta with a little vanilla; add honey or sugar, a pat of butter, and milk.) Here are some other things you can do with leftover polenta:

1. Pour softened polenta in a bowl. Cover it with slices or crumbles of Gorgonzola cheese, grate over a little Parmesan, and add toasted breadcrumbs and chopped parsley mixed with some fresh marjoram. This is comforting in its goodness and simplicity.

2. To make a straightforward gratin, cut firm polenta into planks about 3/4 inch thick, cover them with tomato sauce, and add cheese such as Gorgonzola, Parmesan, fresh or smoked mozzarella, or a mixture of all three. Meat eaters might want to add sausage. Bake in a 375-degree oven until bubbly and hot, about twenty minutes.

3. Fry firm polenta in one pan and heat tomato sauce in another. Spoon the sauce over the polenta and add grated cheese.

4. Reheat polenta and serve with sautéed mushrooms (page 164) to which you've added some diced tomato, fresh or canned.

Moky McKelvey finishes his dish by strewing pieces of prosciutto over all at the end. Leave it out and you have a good vegetarian dinner. Greens cook down so much that you might as well use an entire bunch. If there are any left over, use them to make the green panini with roasted peppers and Gruyère cheese (page 68).

polenta (page 64)

1 tablespoon olive oil

1 small onion, thinly sliced

2 garlic cloves, finely chopped or pressed

3 or 4 big handfuls chard, kale, or other
   cooking greens, leaves removed from
   the stems, rinse and torn

salt and pepper

⅓ cup water or chicken broth

a few drops red wine vinegar

3 slices of prosciutto, cut into strips
   (optional)

Asiago or Parmesan cheese for grating

1. Make the polenta and pour it into a lightly oiled bowl to set.

2. Meanwhile, heat the olive oil in a 10-inch cast-iron skillet over medium heat. When hot, add the onion. Give a stir and cook until the onion is wilted, about 8 minutes, adding the garlic halfway through. Add the greens, sprinkle them with ½ teaspoon salt, and pour in the water or chicken stock. Cover and cook until the greens are wilted and tender, from 8 to 15 minutes, depending on the type of greens used. Sprinkle with vinegar and add the prosciutto, if using. Let rest while you turn out the polenta. Cut polenta into slices and arrange them on your plate, cover with the greens, and grate the cheese over all.

When I thought of Sam Harvey tossing frozen vegetables into his grits, corn came to mind. Of course, it's corn going into corn, but why not contrast the kernels with the grains? Instead of adding the corn to the polenta, I sautéed it with a half-dozen shrimp, lots of scallions, and cilantro. With a large pan to convey plenty of heat to the frozen corn, it should end up defrosted and cooked by the time the shrimp are done.

polenta (page 64)

1½ tablespoons olive oil or
   oil and butter, mixed

4 scallions, including some of the
   greens, chopped

1 cup frozen corn

6 shrimp (defrosted if frozen),
   peeled and deveined

salt and pepper

2 tablespoons chopped cilantro

1. Start the polenta. While it's cooking, heat the olive oil in a 10-inch skillet. When hot, add the scallions, corn, and shrimp. Season with salt and freshly ground pepper to taste, and sauté over high heat, jerking the pan back and forth to turn the shrimp. When the shrimp are pink and firm to the touch the corn should be done. Taste to be sure. Add the cilantro.

2. Serve yourself a bowl of polenta and cover with the shrimp and corn and more black pepper.

GREEN PANINI WITH ROASTED
PEPPERS AND GRUYÈRE CHEESE

If you're going to use fresh spinach, you might as well look to more pungent greens like broccoli rabe, mustard, or turnip greens. And break them down Southern style, that is, cook them until they're really tender. Mustard greens have more punch than spinach, and a bunch yields twice as much, giving you enough for two or three hefty sandwiches. If you're wary of them, know that when mustard greens are cooked until tender, they are as mild and delicious as can be.

1 bunch mustard greens, leaves
  cut off the stems and washed
  but not dried
salt and pepper
red pepper flakes, a few pinches
1 garlic clove, pressed or minced
pepper sauce or red wine vinegar
2 pieces ciabatta, or your favorite
  rustic bread
olive oil
grated Gruyère or fontina cheese
roasted bell pepper cut into
  wide strips
Dijon mustard

1. Put the mustard greens in a pot over high heat with the water that clings to the leaves plus ½ cup. Sprinkle with ½ teaspoon salt, the pepper flakes, and cover. Once the leaves have collapsed, reduce the heat to medium and cook until they're tender when you taste one, about 7 minutes. Drain, then squeeze the excess water out of the greens. Put them in a bowl and season with additional salt, if needed, pepper, the garlic, and pepper sauce or vinegar to taste.

2. Slather the outside of the bread with olive oil. Cover one slice of the bread (the dry side) with cheese, pile on a half or a third of the greens, and add the pepper strips. Spread the top slice with Dijon mustard, then cover.

3. Cook in your panini maker or in a skillet until the bread is crispy and the cheese melts. When a wave of melted cheese hits the hot surface, there's a bonus tang, but don't let it burn. Slice it diagonally—it's easier to eat that way and it looks jaunty, too.

ENGLISH MUFFIN WITH (SPICELESS) RAGU AND SHARP CHEDDAR

Feel free to add spice. Well, not spice, exactly, but herbs —oregano, minced rosemary, torn basil leaves, chopped parsley. They do make everything taste so much more interesting. And if you have tapenade on hand, spread some over the toasted muffin before adding the cheese.

1 English muffin

grated sharp Cheddar cheese

¾ cup tomato sauce (page 230) or ragu, warmed

pepper

chopped fresh herbs

Toast the muffin, then lightly cover both halves with cheese. Divide the tomato sauce between the two halves, cover with a little more cheese, and heat in a toaster oven until the cheese starts to bubble and melt. Season with pepper and liberal pinches of chopped herbs.

These chile-dusted potatoes are
simple and good. Use pure ground
chile, such as New Mexican *molido,*
or whatever your favorite chile substance is, and add it once the potatoes are tender so that it doesn't burn

1 or 2 russet potatoes

olive oil or canola oil

salt

ground red chile (New Mexican
molido), smoked paprika, or
ground chipotle

and take on a bitter taste. These are
excellent with cooked greens (chard, spinach, and kale) and all kinds of sauces
(garlic mayonnaise and romesco sauce), fried eggs, and alongside chicken or
meat. They'd also be a great addition to the breakfast burrito (page 80).

1. Preheat the oven to 400 degrees. Lightly oil a baking dish, such as a
   ceramic gratin dish or a sheet pan, as potatoes tend to stick.

2. Neatly peel the potatoes; cut them in half lengthwise and then into
   quarters lengthwise to make long pieces. Toss them with a teaspoon
   or two of oil and several pinches of salt so that they're well coated
   but not dripping with oil. Make a single layer of potatoes in your dish
   and bake until a pale gold crust has formed and the flesh feels tender
   when pierced with a knife, about 25 minutes.

3. Remove and sprinkle with chile, starting with ¼ teaspoon and adding
   more, to taste; add additional salt, also to taste.

For fans of Southwestern flavors, it's hard to find a better grilled cheese than one that includes a long, roasted green chile.

1 or 2 roasted long green chiles or
   poblano chiles, below
2 slices bread
grated or sliced cheese to cover, such
   as Monterrey Jack or Muenster
chopped cilantro
butter or olive oil

1. Remove the stem, skin, and seeds from the roasted chile(s), then tear the flesh into long strips.

2. Cover one piece of bread with enough cheese to reach nearly to the edge. Add the chile, chopped cilantro, and more cheese. Top with the second piece of bread and brush with olive oil. Put it in a hot skillet and cook over medium-low heat until the bread is crisp and the cheese is melted. Press on it a few times with a spatula while it's cooking. When golden brown on the bottom, turn it over and cook the second side until golden brown.

HOW TO ROAST GREEN CHILE

Regardless of whether its sweet or hot, you can roast a pepper by turning on your burner, putting the pepper right in the flame, and leaving it there until the skin is charred. You'll have to turn it this way and that to make sure the whole chile is hit with the flame. Drop it in a bowl and cover with a plate to steam for 10 minutes or longer. Next, pull off the charred skins (try to avoid just washing away the flavor under running water, which is easier), slit them, and scrape out the seeds unless you want more heat, in which case, leave them in.

The Quaker cowboy selected mashed potatoes with green chile as one of his eat-alone dishes. This thick and hearty stew retains that timeless combination but is more of a main dish. You could mash it, if you like, or add another cup or two of liquid to turn it into a soup. The sour cream softens the chile's heat and brings everything into a delicious and balanced mouthful.

1 or 2 long green chiles or poblano chiles, roasted and peeled (see page 71)
1 tablespoon sunflower seed oil or other vegetable oil
1 small onion, diced
½ teaspoon ground coriander
¼ teaspoon ground cumin
1 garlic clove, minced
1 large russet or 5 smaller potatoes (a scant pound) peeled and chopped into 1½-inch chunks
salt and pepper
1 cup water or chicken stock
sour cream to finish
chopped cilantro to finish

1. Chop the chiles coarsely. Heat the oil in a wide pot; add the onion and cook over medium-low heat, stirring frequently until softened, about 4 minutes. Add the coriander, cumin, garlic, and potatoes, followed by the chile along with ½ teaspoon salt and give a stir. Cook together for a few minutes, then add the water or stock. Bring to a boil, then lower the heat to a simmer.

2. Cover and cook until the potatoes are completely softened, about 25 minutes. Taste for salt and season with pepper. At this point you can mash the potatoes, or at least a few of them to give the dish a creamy sort of background, if desired.

3. Pour into a bowl; add a dollop of sour cream and the chopped cilantro.

TOMATILLO SALSA

This is enough tangy green sauce to assemble chilaquiles verdes for the course of a week, which is great if you're the kind of person who likes to eat the same thing over and over. Make half as much if that thought doesn't appeal to you.

2 pounds tomatillos

2 or more jalapeños (depending on whether they're hot), stemmed and quartered, seeds left in for a hotter sauce

1 bunch green onions, including a little green, roughly chopped

1 large garlic clove

handful of cilantro, roughly chopped

salt

3 cups water or chicken broth

sunflower seed or vegetable oil

1. Remove the tomatillo husks and rinse the fruits. Put them in a skillet or on a sheet pan; broil until charred in places, about 10 to 15 minutes in all. Give the pan a shake every 4 minutes or so, making sure that the tomatillos brown and blister in places.

2. Throw the tomatillos in a blender with the jalapeños, green onions, garlic, cilantro, $\frac{1}{2}$ teaspoon salt, and the water or broth. Purée until smooth.

3. Our solo cook stopped at this point and stashed his sauce in the refrigerator, but you can take the raw edge off the garlic and onions by briefly cooking the sauce: heat a tablespoon or two of oil in a pot or skillet, add the sauce and cook at a slow boil while stirring for five minutes. Let cool, then taste for salt.

Chilaquiles, a soul-satisfying dish, is assembled on the stove within minutes once you have your tomatillo salsa. Amounts of cheese and sour cream and all of that are entirely up to you, and if you like, you can top it all with a fried egg. The most important thing is to not let the chips stay in the sauce so long that they get soggy, so you'll want to have everything grated, crumbled, and chopped, plus a warm plate.

1 to 1½ cups tomatillo salsa (page 73)
2 handfuls tortilla chips, preferably thick Mexican-style chips
a handful grated Monterey Jack
a little crumbled cheese for sharpness, such as Cotija, feta, or Parmesan
cooked chorizo sausage (optional)
sour cream or Mexican *crema,* loosened with a fork
cilantro leaves, thinly sliced white onion, or pickled onion rings (page 95) for garnish

Choose a skillet that's large enough to hold everything comfortably, such as an 8-inch cast-iron or nonstick pan. Bring the sauce to a boil in the pan, then add the chips and stir them into the sauce with a rubber spatula. Get them well coated and, at the most, just slightly softened. Scrape everything onto a heated plate, scatter the cheeses and sausage (if using) over the top, then drizzle over sour cream and finish with a flourish of cilantro and sliced onion. Enjoy without a moment's hesitation.

DAN'S SPICY TAPENADE

MAKES 1 HEAPING CUP

This is the ingredient that has guided so much of Dan Welch's cooking, whether for himself alone or for others. If you like tapenade too, you'll find many places to use it. Some suggestions are given below. It keeps for at least a week or two in the refrigerator.

½ pound mixed black olives (about 1½ cups)

¼ cup capers, briefly rinsed

4 anchovies (unless you're a vegetarian)

¼ cup good olive oil or more, as needed to loosen the mixture

2 small garlic cloves, finely chopped

grated zest and juice of 1 large lemon

1 teaspoon red pepper flakes or a few twists of black pepper

1 tablespoon chopped parsley

Remove the pits from the olives if they aren't already pitted. You should end up with about a cup. Chop them by hand or in a food processor, leaving the olives a bit coarse. Add the rest of the ingredients except the parsley, and pulse, leaving some texture; you don't want mush. You might need to add a little additional olive oil to loosen the mixture. Stir in the parsley and you're ready to go.

USES FOR TAPENADE

Spread on crackers with white bean purée, goat cheese, or nothing at all.

Slather on bread in a grilled cheese sandwich or just about any panini.

Serve with hard-boiled eggs and little tomatoes.

Toss with egg pasta, using extra oil or some of the hot pasta water.

Serve with raw vegetables.

Serve with the seared tuna (page 184).

The grilled cheese sandwich changes form here, becoming open faced and including, along with the cheese, a thick layer of tapenade, sliced tomatoes, and cucumbers, all piled on old-world *levain* bread. It's too messy to hold, so you might want to add a second slice of bread, toasted or not, to eat the sandwich in a more or less mannerly fashion. Serve with pickled onion rings (page 95) and coleslaw.

1 or 2 slices levain bread or other rustic bread

Muenster, mozzarella, aged Cheddar, or your favorite cheese, thinly sliced

Dan's spicy tapenade (page 75)

sliced tomatoes

chopped cilantro and jalapeño chile

sliced cucumbers

Lay the cheese on the bread and toast it in a toaster oven until the cheese is bubbly and starting to melt. Remove and spread a thick layer of tapenade over the cheese, then add a layer of sliced tomatoes. Chop the cilantro and chiles together, sprinkle over the tomatoes, then top with cucumbers. You probably won't need salt because of the tapenade. Add a second layer of bread if you like, toasted or not. Slice in half. Have a lot of napkins nearby.

SALSA FRESCA

MAKES ABOUT 1/2 CUP

Although it's easily purchased, those who love salsa and find it indispensable often prefer to make their own. This is the one to eat with Dan's poisoned eggs, a burrito, or stirred into a bowl of pinto beans. It's also for chips. Although salsa fresca will keep, it's much better eaten sooner than later.

2 medium ripe red tomatoes

1 jalapeño chile or serrano, for more heat and more flavor

10 cilantro sprigs, chopped

2 or more tablespoons finely diced white or red onion

salt

fresh lime juice, to taste

a few teaspoons cold water or olive oil

Cut the tomatoes in half around the equator, pull out the seeds with your fingers, then chop the tomatoes into small pieces and put them in a bowl. Finely dice either chile, including the seeds, to give the salsa more heat. Add them to the tomatoes along with the cilantro, onion, and a few pinches of salt. Stir in the lime juice to taste and add enough water or olive oil to loosen the mixture.

MAKES ABOUT 5 CUPS

Once you've got cooked pinto beans on hand, you can enjoy a hot bowl of them laced with a salsa fresca (page 77) use them to make a Frito pie (page 32) or drain them, mash them up a bit, and put them in a burrito or turn them into a soup. You can also freeze some for another time if you've made more than you can contemplate eating over the course of a few days.

2 cups dry pinto beans, rinsed

1 medium onion, chopped

2 garlic cloves, chopped

1 teaspoon dried oregano

salt

1 teaspoon smoked paprika, plus more, to taste

Cotija or Cheddar cheese, for serving

If you want your beans to have a smoky flavor, stir in some smoked Spanish paprika, starting with a teaspoon and working up from there.

1. To speed the cooking time, first cover the beans with boiling water and let them stand for an hour or just while you chop your onion and gather ingredients. Then, drain the beans.

2. Put the beans in a soup pot, cover with 8 cups (2 quarts) water, and boil for 10 minutes. Remove any foam that collects on the surface, then add the onion, garlic, and oregano. Lower the heat so the beans barely boil and continue cooking, partially covered, until they're tender, 1 to 1½ hours, adding 2 teaspoons salt about halfway through.

3. When the beans are done, taste for salt again. Add smoked paprika to taste if using. Serve in bowls with their broth, fresh tomato salsa, and a sprinkling of cheese, such as Cotija or Cheddar.

SOME VARIATIONS

1. Slowly fry a sliced onion in two tablespoons oil with several pinches dried oregano and 1 teaspoon ground cumin. Then add the beans and water, and cook.

2. Add a dried red chile to the pot while the beans cook. You can stem and seed the chile first or not.

3. If you're handy with a pressure cooker, skip the soaking and cook the beans with the aromatics at 15 pounds for 25 minutes. Drop the pressure, remove the lid, and check to make sure they're done. If not, return the lid, bring the pot back up to pressure, and cook 5 minutes longer.

This is a simple burrito consisting of eggs softly scrambled in butter and enfolded in a big warm whole-wheat tortilla flecked with bits of bran. Leave it plain or add your favorite salsa.

You'll need two skillets, one for the tortilla and the other for the eggs. You'll be warming the tortilla and making the eggs at the same time. It's no big deal.

1 large tortilla, preferably whole wheat

2 or 3 fresh eggs

salt

1 tablespoon butter

grated Jack or Cheddar cheese or
    crumbled goat cheese

salsa

1. Warm a skillet large enough to hold a tortilla over medium heat. Add the tortilla when you start to cook the eggs. Keep an eye on the tortilla as the eggs cook and turn it once so that it heats on both sides.

2. Meanwhile, beat the eggs with a few pinches of salt and a tablespoon of water. Melt the butter in a second, smaller pan. Once the butter has ceased to foam, turn the heat to medium low and pour in the eggs. Cook, stirring slowly but constantly, until the eggs are almost as done as you like, then throw the cheese over the top and remove them from the heat.

3. Slide the tortilla onto a plate, mound the eggs on half of the tortilla, and add salsa, if using. Fold in half or roll it up. Eat with warm beans.

This rustic asparagus Polonaise is so very good that two pounds aren't too much. But we'll go with one pound here (preferably thick asparagus) for those who don't want leftovers. You can always double the recipe if you do. It's not hard to polish the whole thing off for dinner.

1 pound asparagus, rinsed
olive oil
salt and pepper
1 piece of sourdough or other
   country style bread
1 or 2 eggs

THE VINAIGRETTE

1 teaspoon coarse mustard
1 tablespoon red wine vinegar
salt
3 tablespoons olive oil

1. Heat the oven to 400 degrees F.

2. Rinse the asparagus and peel the stems if thick. If thin, snap them off where they break easily, then trim the ends. Toss with a teaspoon or so of olive oil to moisten, season well with salt and pepper, and lay in a baking dish. Roast, turning once every 10 minutes, until tender and colored in places, 25 to 30 minutes.

3. While the asparagus is cooking, put the bread in the oven to crisp, then tear it into small pieces. Put the egg(s) in a saucepan, cover with cold water, and bring to a boil. After 1 minute turn off the heat, cover the pot, and let stand for 6 minutes. Drain, then peel and chop.

4. Whisk the mustard with the vinegar and ¼ teaspoon salt, then whisk in olive oil. Taste and correct for tartness.

5. Lay the asparagus on a plate. Cover with the egg, scatter the bread and spoon the vinaigrette over all. Finish with cracked pepper.

The important thing in the idea of this asparagus salad is to keep the dressing away from the asparagus until you plan to eat it, otherwise the vinegar will turn it an increasingly dull shade of green. Make the

2 pounds asparagus

salt

olive oil

mustard vinaigrette (from the previous recipe)

same dressing as in the previous recipe, only doubling the amount since you'll be eating it longer. Put it in a jar so that you can shake it up each time you use it. Or skip the dressing and instead drizzle olive oil and squeeze a lemon over the asparagus.

1. Rinse the asparagus well and peel the stalks if they are thick; otherwise, snap the stalks where they break first, then trim the ends.

2. Bring a large skillet of water to a boil and add salt. Add the asparagus, or as much will fit comfortably, and cook at a gentle boil until a piece tastes done when you cut it, anywhere from 4 to 8 minutes depending on its size.

3. When the asparagus is done, put it on a clean towel to drain, then put it in a dish and toss it with oil to coat lightly. Cover and refrigerate. When it's time for that asparagus salad, take what you want to eat, shake the jar of dressing, and drizzle it over the asparagus.

CHAPTER 5

Saved by Sardines,
Rescued by Pasta

*"I take a tin of sardines, mix it with lemon juice and mayonnaise,
and make a sandwich. That's dinner."*

—A Tassajara workshop participant

ONE DECEMBER WE PUT TWO CANS OF SARDINES and some crackers in the
glove compartment of the car, a suggestion from one of our interviewees, and took off for a two-week road trip to California. When
we got back to New Mexico, I returned the sardines to their place on
the shelf and crumbled up the crackers for the birds.

Years earlier the same thing had happened when Marion
Cunningham and I took a road trip from California to the
Southwest and found ourselves unable to resist the roadside attrac-
tions. Although we had the option of eating those wholesome
sardines we had brought along for lunch at roadside rest stops, they
couldn't compete with the lure of warm hearth breads and hand
pies baked in the native clay hornos, and those cold Heath Blizzards

offered every so many miles on I-40. Once home, the sardines were returned to the cupboard.

Actually I do like sardines, but not enough, apparently. Still, they would be good to have on hand in an emergency, which is why we had them in the first place.

But what kind of emergency? Say you've ended up in Austin, Nevada (population, a few; location, remote), on New Year's Eve after the only café has closed. Or, you've dropped your keys in the mountain stream where you were fly-fishing, and you have nothing to eat while you wait for the tow truck except that can of sardines you found tucked away in your knapsack. Or you're on a long road trip, just like we were, and you hunger for an alternative to the usual roadside options. Situations like these are sardine-warranting emergencies and, of course, so is being snowed in and having eaten through everything else in your cupboard. In fact, sardines, along with pasta and canned tomatoes, are three trusty cupboard foods that are good to keep on hand.

Sardines are also good to know about when you're a hungry student on a modest budget. Having burned out on sardines when he was in art school, Patrick won't go near them, but there are many who turn faithfully to these and other canned fish when rustling up their solitary meals. One woman explains her approach like this.

"I take a tin of sardines, mix it with lemon juice and mayonnaise, and make a sandwich. That's dinner." And it's actually pretty good, especially on toasted rye bread.

An Ohioan dictates her sardine recipe as follows: "Open a can, pour in balsamic vinegar, sprinkle over herbs and dip bread into it. It's delicious." While a third woman creates a whole meal with sardines at the center of the plate. "Take canned sardines," she says, "they must

be boneless and skinless, add lemon juice and olive oil, and serve with sauerkraut and parsley potatoes."

Sardines, by the way, along with herrings, mackerel, salmon and other fish in a can, provide an extremely affordable way to consume fish that's rich in those sought-after Omega-3s. And if you eat the soft little bones, you get calcium, too.

Recently I was on a panel with Paul Johnson, the author of *Fish Forever* and one of the most knowledgeable people around when it comes to fish. Someone from the audience who knew of this project turned the tables and asked all of us what we eat when we eat alone. Paul was visibly sheepish about his answer, which, he finally announced in a confessional tone, "Sardines. On rye crackers." When I asked him later why he was embarrassed by his answer, especially given that sardines were one of the most frequent responses to the eat-alone question, he said, "Because they aren't fresh!"

And I guess if you're in the fresh fish business, you might feel a little awkward about eating canned. Who knew? But then, that's how I feel about vegetables: frozen won't do, although I'm pretty sure I have some peas somewhere in my freezer.

Sardines on toast is what I turn to, although smoked herring might end up the same way. I toast a hefty slice of whole-wheat or sourdough bread, lay the fish over it, gently press it into the toast, then add a squeeze of fresh lemon juice, some sea salt, and coarse pepper. If they were packed in water, I drizzle some olive oil over the fish and add a little minced parsley to freshen it. I cut the toast into quarters and savor each one. Pickled onions are good here, too, and you can easily make a slew of them to have on hand to make all kinds of foods lively and pretty.

When it came to fish in a can, salmon was mentioned only once, when Marsha Weiner talked about making her grandmother's salmon cakes. Due to a special, I had quite a few large cans of salmon in my cupboard that I hadn't gotten around to using until Marsha sent us her grandmother's recipe. Although the idea of eating canned salmon did not, understandably, go over well with a bunch of chef friends from Seattle with whom I enthusiastically shared the recipe, I can tell you that a salmon cake is a great eat-alone item. Once again, if you want to eat wild rather than farmed salmon but can't always find it or pay its hefty price, canned Alaskan salmon is very affordable, is wild, and doesn't go bad. But be warned, it's not always very pretty stuff, especially the cheap kind. It's not particularly pink (though the more expensive brands are), it doesn't necessarily come in distinct, big chunks like tuna does, and you will no doubt find some tiny little vertebrae when you turn the fish into a bowl. But don't let any of this stop you. Just pick out the bones and know that by the time you've assembled your cakes and got them crusty and golden in a skillet, none of this will matter in the least. They're delicious.

Tuna, not surprisingly, is also a common answer to the solo dinner question—canned tuna, that is. More serious cooks and eaters go for fresh, which takes very little time to cook but is fairly costly. People we met in Europe frequently mentioned tuna in olive oil as the backbone ingredient of their meals, as do friends in the U.S. One cook was especially enthusiastic about his bean and tuna dish. After making it clear that he never does the same thing twice, he avowed that he liked what he had recently cooked so much that he would do it again. What he did was heat a tin of borlotti beans in a pan with olive oil and garlic, squeeze in a bit of tomato paste for color, and add a small dollop of the spicy Tunisian chile paste, harissa, for flavor.

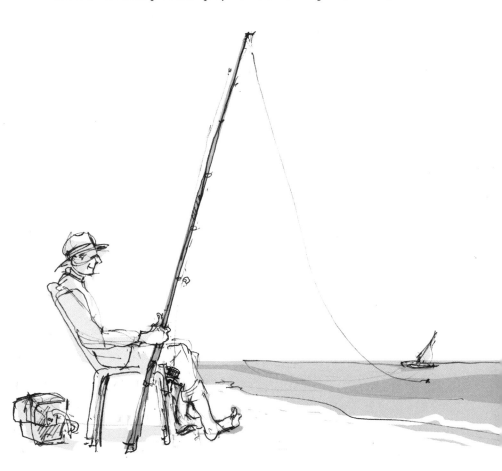

Then he flaked a small tin of Spanish tuna over the beans and added a scraping of Parmesan cheese.

"Rich, filling, and interesting" was his assessment. Of course this brings to mind those Italian salads made with canned tuna in oil and borlotti or cannellini beans mixed with thinly sliced onions, capers, and vinegar. Such salads also make a good solo meal, albeit not a warm one but a good option for summer.

Tuna and chile appear in one fellow's (yes, Dan the monk's) tuna sandwich, in which the canned fish is mixed with lots of chopped jalapeños and cilantro as well as capers, plenty of mayo, and, though this is optional for some reason, celery. All of this gets heaped onto a large slice of toasted levain bread. More simply, you can purée tuna (and water-packed will be fine), with mustard, mayonnaise, capers, and not too much garlic, and eat it on crackers for a meal, or before one. I learned to make tuna spread when I cooked for a much older woman who thought that a tuna spread made a terrific cocktail canapé, and it does, especially when you need a tasty little spread at the last minute. Spread it on toast or a cracker, add extra capers or a sliced pimento-stuffed olive, and it can pony up to a martini or a salad of sliced tomatoes, green beans, and a hard-cooked egg.

Regardless of what fish is in the tin, it's best when it comes packed in olive oil. It's much tastier than water and, for that matter, canola or soy oil. Mustard sauce isn't necessary, although some sardines come that way. You can always add mustard later to your toast or cracker. But the olive oil is good. As it also picks up the flavor of the fish—or shellfish— it can even be used to dress that other staple food that rescues lone eaters from hunger on a regular basis, and that is pasta. One fellow shared his method for making a meal of linguini with the oil remaining from smoked oysters.

"When I've eaten a tin of smoked oysters," he says, "I save the oil in the can. The next day I cook up linguini using the al dente taste test, then drain it. I leave the can on top of the hot pasta for a minute to extract the entire yummy oyster flavor, then pour it over the noodles."

Taking a tip from him, one night I found myself pouring the olive oil from a can of Spanish sardines over a salad of potatoes (left over from Patrick's seven-at-once fuel-saving effort), celery, hard-cooked egg, and green olives. A good dish. And the sardines went on toast for an appetizer. Another solo cook, who didn't save his oil, downed his canned oysters, oil and all, with Tabasco sauce and beer. But this was an appetizer. Pasta came later, or so he claimed.

Dried pasta has already been made for you. That's the big time-saver. But water has to come to a boil, the pasta has to cook, and during this interval you might as well do something—open that can of tuna, chop herbs, dice tomatoes, separate a head of cauliflower into little florets. Pasta offers a good compromise between cooking everything from scratch and not cooking anything at all. But despite the ease with which this can happen (and pasta's short but popular history in America as a standby dish), it wasn't mentioned nearly as often as we thought it might be. Perhaps it's the carbs.

Spaghetti with tuna, however, is a dish that draws upon these two basic cupboard foods—canned fish and noodles. "I keep a small can of Mediterranean tuna on hand," writes the author of this recipe. "You bring water to a boil, add salt, and drop in boxed pasta—spaghetti or linguini. While it cooks, put tuna in a skillet and break it up. Add chopped fresh garlic and hot pepper flakes. A minute before the pasta is cooked, put chopped arugula in the skillet to wilt. Drain the pasta and add it to the skillet with plenty of freshly squeezed lemon juice. Have it with cold white wine or rosé. A good summer dish."

When it did come up, though, the approaches to a box of spaghetti were generally wholesome and good. That is, vegetables were included and often in quantity. One clear winner is **green penne with potatoes and broccoli** recommended by a bachelor who cooks, whom we met on one of our food trips.

"In more or less equal portions, you're going to cook penne rigate (the quills with grooves running the length of each noodle), broccoli, and potatoes. You're going to cut the vegetables into bite-size pieces and throw everything simultaneously into boiling salted water. You're going to break up anchovies (another tinned fish), and heat them in a skillet with olive oil, freshly chopped garlic, and pepper flakes. Then you're going to toss it all together. You get a green coating on everything. Add grated Parmesan and you have a great dinner."

This is an excellent dish. And so is **hungry man's pasta** proposed by another traveling acquaintance. "What I do when I'm really hungry is I cook Rusticella pasta. It's pasta Abruzzi style. I put jarred arugula sauce—it's got arugula, almonds, and anchovies in it—and add olive oil." If you can find some of this sauce, you will be well advised to do the same. If not, you can make the sauce with ease.

Joe Simone, another fellow traveler through Puglia in southeastern Italy, who is also a chef, described pasta as a trustworthy standby food. His approach is to toss **pasta with cauliflower**, toasted breadcrumbs, chile pepper, and plenty of "good olive oil." Admittedly, we were in Puglia with a lot of others on a quest for good olive oil, but Joe would always want to use good olive oil no matter where he'd be cooking. Indeed, it makes everything taste better. He adds, "This is a great dish for anyone, and it doesn't have to be eaten alone. In fact it's better shared, but then, a lot of things are."

Our affable neighbor, Ken Khune, regularly devotes an hour or two to cooking dinner for himself and his wife, but when he's eating alone, he reports that pasta is likely to be his number one fallback food. "Most of the time I just toss **spaghetti with sun-dried tomatoes**, plus black olives, capers, parsley, lots of garlic, and, of course, good olive oil. But you can add sautéed shrimp for a little extra pizzazz," he suggests. "Yeah, baby!"

Similarly, an importer of rare Chinese teas also turns to simple pasta with robust and fiery attributes. "As I'm batching it these days," Sebastian Beckwirth writes, "I often do the quick and delicious penne or linguini arrabiata with plenty of chili, garlic, oregano, and olive oil!" And finally, Cliff Wright, again, who commands an enormous repertoire of complicated culinary possibilities, says, "When I eat alone and I'm not eating a combination of leftovers, the two kinds of dishes I like to make for myself are spaghetti with a little bit of meat, like pancetta or leftover something, or spaghetti tossed with finely chopped vegetables, maybe an egg or some Parmigiano tossed in."

I imagine that the simplicity of such pastas as Cliff's would be a comfort to a person who is constantly cooking what are often very complex dishes. What a relief to turn to something so straightforward as hot pasta tossed with an egg and some good cheese. Have a sardine on a cracker with a clump of watercress while the water is boiling, and you've got a real meal.

Perhaps we shouldn't be surprised, but only one woman said that she cooked pasta when eating alone, and this is a woman who says she always has three vegetable dishes at dinner. Sylvia Thompson, a garden-centric cook and writer, says, "Now that I'm mostly vegetarian, I'd say it's pasta twice a week. Lots of mushrooms and pasta. Cheese and pasta. Herbs and pasta." Describing her most recent pasta meal—saffron fettuccine sauced with a sauté of sliced mushrooms, kalamata olives, and leaves of fresh baby spinach, loosened with canned crushed tomatoes—she adds, "I might not have added the spinach," she said, "but it was going to be lost if I didn't cook it tonight. Actually, the little green flags in the dish were quite nice, but essentially it's mushrooms and olives with the crushed tomatoes."

So it appears that with the exception of Sylvia, pasta, with all its carbs and happy affinity for (good) olive oil, and despite its affinity for vegetables, is now a man's food.

SARDINES ON TOAST

It needn't be sardines, you know. There's also canned herring, smoked trout, mackerel—all kinds of fish that come in cans. Here's one way to enjoy them. The bones are a good source of calcium, they say, but sardines do come without them.

1 or 2 pieces of rye or whole-grain bread
mayonnaise
mustard
1 can of sardines or other fish
pepper
half a lemon
pickled onion rings (below) or a few thin slices of sweet onion

Toast the bread. Spread it lightly with mayonnaise and a little mustard. Lay sardines over the toast and gently press them into it so they'll stick. Grind pepper and squeeze the lemon juice over all. Cover with pickled onion rings or thinly sliced sweet onions, slice into quarters, and eat.

PICKLED ONION RINGS

Pickled onions can be ready in 15 minutes, keep for days, and bless all with their cheerful color (if they were red to start with) and vinegary tang. Their texture softens a little each day, so you don't want to have too many on hand if it's just you.

1 red or white onion
½ teaspoon salt
1 teaspoon sugar
apple cider vinegar or rice wine vinegar

Peel and then slice an onion into thin rounds. Separate the rounds and put them in a bowl. Toss with the salt and sugar, then pour vinegar over to nearly cover. Add water, about a fifth of the total amount of liquid, to cover. Swish the onions around to dissolve the sugar and salt. It will take about 15 minutes for them to color up. Store in the refrigerator.

MARSHA'S SALMON CAKES

Canned salmon can sit on your shelf and wait patiently for you to get it into view. One small (7½-ounce) can makes 2 good-sized salmon cakes or 3 pretty-good-sized ones—too many for most people at one sitting, but you can have them several meals apart. Once I put a leftover cooked salmon cake in the fridge and found it a few days later. It was good, even cold. I had it that way with a spritz of fresh lemon juice, horseradish, and pickled onion rings (page 95) over a bed of lightly dressed arugula.

1 (7½-ounce) can salmon, about 1 cup

1½ tablespoons minced scallions or onion

2 tablespoons chopped parsley

½ teaspoon grated lemon zest

1 tablespoon mayonnaise

½ to 1 teaspoon mustard

salt and pepper

1 egg, small if you have one

½ cup plus 2 tablespoons breadcrumbs, fresh or dried

olive oil for frying

1. Open the can of salmon, pour off its liquid, then turn it into a bowl. Break it up with a fork and pick out any little bones. Add the scallions, parsley, lemon zest, mayonnaise, and mustard, and mix everything together lightly with a fork. Season to taste with salt and freshly ground pepper. Stir the egg into the fish with a fork, followed by the breadcrumbs.

2. Heat a cast-iron or nonstick skillet and coat it with a film of oil. Shape the salmon mixture into patties. Slide them into the hot pan and cook about 5 minutes on each side. They should be brown and crisp on the outside, soft and moist within. Serve on a bed of arugula with lemon wedges, horseradish, mayonnaise, or sour cream.

1. Add 3 tablespoons chopped cilantro (instead of, or along with, the parsley) and ½ minced green jalapeño chile. Serve with jarred or homemade tomatillo salsa (page 73).

2. Replace the lemon with lime and serve with sour cream and lime wedges on a bed of thinly sliced napa cabbage.

TUNA SPREAD WITH CAPERS

This makes a nice change from the usual tuna spread. Water-packed tuna is fine here, as you will be adding olive oil.

1 can tuna, drained

1 small garlic clove, coarsely chopped

2 tablespoons olive oil

3 anchovies

1 teaspoon mustard

2 tablespoons mayonnaise

salt and pepper

zest and juice of 1 small lemon

1 tablespoon capers, plus extra for garnish

a few pinches chopped parsley, thyme leaves, or snipped chives

Drop the first 6 ingredients in a food processor and pulse until well blended. Add a few pinches of salt, lemon zest, and a teaspoon of lemon juice, and pulse to combine. Scrape the spread into a bowl, stir in the capers, and season it to taste with pepper. Spread the tuna over toast or crackers and garnish with the additional capers and a pinch of fresh green herbs.

It's waiting for the water to boil that takes longest in this very satisfying pasta—just time enough to throw together a salad or cook a vegetable. Half of a 7-ounce can of tuna in olive oil will make an ample dish for one. Use the second half for a tuna salad, spread, or sandwich. Crisp breadcrumbs are scattered over the pasta at the end to give the dish a nice crunchy finish.

breadcrumbs from one slice of bread

2 tablespoons olive oil, in all

3 to 4 ounces whole wheat or
white spaghetti

salt and pepper

½ can tuna in olive oil (about
3½ ounces)

1 tablespoon capers, rinsed

pinch of red pepper flakes

1 garlic clove, minced or pressed

1 lemon, zest and juice to taste

chopped parsley

1. Put the breadcrumbs in a small skillet with half the oil or butter on medium heat. Cook, stirring every so often, for about 5 minutes, or until crisp and golden, then turn off the heat.

2. Bring a large pot of water to boil, then add in plenty of salt and the spaghetti. Give it a stir and boil until al dente, 8 to 10 minutes. Keep tasting until it's as done as you like.

3. While the spaghetti is cooking, heat the remaining oil in a skillet wide enough to hold the finished dish. Add the tuna, the capers, pepper flakes and garlic, then grind in plenty of pepper. Cook over medium heat for a few minutes, breaking up the tuna with a fork.

4. When the spaghetti is done, lift it out of the water with tongs and transfer it directly to the pan with tuna, allowing some water to drip into the pan. Add a few pinches of lemon zest plus the parsley and toss well with a little lemon juice. Pile the spaghetti into a warm bowl, then scatter the breadcrumbs over the top.

What makes this dish green are all the little bits of broccoli that break off into the pasta water. As for amounts, judge for yourself by eye what you think you want to eat, in what proportion, and if you want leftovers. If you're a huge broccoli fan, use even twice as much. If you're going light on pasta, use fewer noodles. And don't throw up your hands at potatoes and pasta in the same dish—the contrasting soft and firm textures are a pleasure to eat.

1 head or more broccoli, with or without the stem, cut into small florets

2 small potatoes, any kind, peeled and diced into ½-inch chunks

salt and pepper

1 or 2 handfuls penne rigate or smooth penne

olive oil

2 anchovies (optional)

2 garlic cloves, minced or pressed

a few pinches red pepper flakes

1 lemon, zest and juice to taste

Parmesan, Asiago, or Pecorino Romano cheese for grating

1. First, get a big pot of water heating, then cut the vegetables. If using the broccoli stem, peel it thickly, then dice it into chunks about the same size as the potatoes.

2. When the water is boiling, add salt, then the broccoli, potatoes, and pasta, and boil until the pasta is done, usually about 8 minutes, but taste it to make sure. The broccoli florets will float to the surface, so you can scoop them out early if you don't want them too soft.

3. Once you've got the vegetables cooking, heat a skillet that will hold everything and add about 3 tablespoons olive oil with the anchovies and mash them into the oil. Add the garlic and pepper flakes, and turn the heat to very low. When the pasta and vegetables are done, scoop them out and add to the pan along with some of the water. Add the lemon zest, toss well, and taste for salt. Season with freshly ground pepper. For sharpness, squeeze in a little of the lemon juice. Transfer to a heated dish and grate cheese over all.

SPAGHETTI WITH SUN-DRIED TOMATOES, OLIVES, AND CAPERS

This hearty spaghetti supper was mentioned at least a few times. One man makes it with sun-dried tomatoes, another with fresh, while a third uses canned. Anchovies are often added, and one lone cook topped his spaghetti with sautéed shrimp. However you approach it, there should be plenty of big lusty flavor from the pepper flakes, olives, garlic—everything, really. These are approximate amounts.

salt

3 to 4 ounces spaghetti

2 tablespoons olive oil

1 large garlic clove, minced or pressed

2 healthy pinches red pepper flakes

3 tablespoons slivered sun-dried tomatoes packed in oil, or about a cup of diced fresh cherry or Roma tomatoes

3 anchovies, finely chopped

2 tablespoons chopped kalamata or Niçoise olives

1 tablespoon capers

3 tablespoons chopped parsley

a few sprigs slivered basil or a teaspoon chopped oregano

grated zest of 1 small lemon, plus juice, to taste

Parmesan cheese for grating

1. Bring a big pot of water to boil for the pasta. When it boils, add plenty of salt and then the spaghetti.

2. While the spaghetti is cooking, chop the rest of the ingredients, including the lemon zest, and put them in a bowl big enough for the finished dish.

3. When the spaghetti is done, drain it, then immediately add it to the bowl and toss. Taste a strand and add more salt or a squeeze of lemon juice, if needed. Add grated cheese to taste.

Following the suggestion of what our hungry man chose for a solo dinner, this is what we came up with. It's rather more pungent and less floral than a pesto made with basil, given the anchovies and arugula, but it does wonders for spaghetti. It will keep for the better part of the week. Toss it with potatoes,

⅓ cup almonds

1 large garlic clove, coarsely chopped

salt and pepper

2 or 3 anchovies

3 cups arugula, fairly well packed,
  but not obsessively

⅓ cup olive oil

3 to 4 ounces spaghetti

Pecorino or Parmesan cheese for grating

spread it on croutons, and use it where you'd use other pestos. This makes enough for one big plate of pasta plus a repeat.

1. Toast the almonds in a toaster oven or regular oven at about 325 degrees F until they smell good, 5 to 8 minutes. Pulse them in a food processor with the garlic and ¼ teaspoon salt until finely ground.

2. Add the anchovies and arugula, and pulse again until smooth. With the motor running, add the olive oil. If needed, add more oil to loosen the mixture. Stop and scrape down the sides. Taste for salt and season with freshly ground pepper.

3. Cook the spaghetti in boiling salted water. Put half of the pesto in a bowl large enough to accommodate the pasta. When the pasta is done, lift it out and into the bowl, allowing some water to drip into it. Toss well. Taste for salt and season with freshly ground pepper. Grate the cheese over the hot, green spaghetti.

SHORT PASTA WITH CAULIFLOWER, PEPPER FLAKES, AND PARSLEY-WALNUT CRUMBS

Cauliflower can be surprisingly bland, so it takes some flavorful items to make this dish sing, which it does. I adore the crunchy bite that crisped breadcrumbs lend to pasta dishes like this one. One night, I used walnuts instead, chopped with garlic and parsley, an even tastier but still crunchy option.

¼ to ½ head cauliflower, as much as you wish to eat, by eye

2 to 4 ounces whole-wheat pasta shapes

salt and pepper

2 tablespoons olive oil

2 tablespoons butter

a few healthy pinches red pepper flakes

a handful parsley leaves

1 large garlic clove

¼ cup walnuts

Asiago or Parmesan cheese, for grating

1. Bring a pot of water to a boil for the cauliflower and pasta. While it's heating, cut the cauliflower into small florets. Dice the core and use it too. When the water boils, add salt and then the cauliflower. Cook until tender-firm—you don't want it mushy—scoop it out and set aside. Add the pasta to the boiling water.

2. While the pasta is cooking, warm the oil, butter, and pepper flakes over medium heat in a skillet large enough to contain the finished dish. Chop the parsley with the garlic and walnuts, then add them to the oil along with the cauliflower. Give a stir and season well with salt and freshly ground pepper. Lower the heat.

3. When the pasta is done, drain, and then add it to the skillet. Turn to coat the pasta and cauliflower with the oil and parsley mixture. Spoon onto a warm pasta plate and grate the cheese over the top.

The couch is a place of solace and comfort for many women, but it can be a challenging choice when eating with animals. When Roz goes to the couch to have dinner while studying Roman antiquities via The History Channel, she says, "I set my food on the coffee table and eat around the cat, which is inevitably in my lap. This makes the eating part a bit tricky, especially if shrimp are involved. Then, it's one for Tiny, two for me, one for Tiny, two for me."

Men and Their Meat

"No steak sauce compares with whiskey."

—James Turrell, *artist and rancher*

"LEE WEEDABAHL'S HOT CORNED BEEF SANDWICHES made him famous in horse parks across the nation," Patrick reminisces. "The sandwiches were simple, gigantic, and delicious. Nothing more than slabs of corned beef pushing ovals of light Jewish rye into a structure resembling a miniature Bilbao. Big sandwiches hand carved by a diminutive smiling man. When I was eight years old, Lee and I were nearly the same size. This is documented in a photo of us wearing matching Coca-Cola patterned shirts. Did he shop in the boy's department? In any case, those sandwiches stayed with me, and when I'm home alone, corned beef is what I make."

These horse park meals have long filtered down into Patrick's culinary repertoire. On numerous occasions I've come home from a trip, opened the door of the fridge, and found myself staring down at a big ruddy chunk of corned beef, a nearly empty jar of horseradish, and an enormous bowl of cooked cabbage and potatoes—and this from a man who was a committed vegetarian for twelve years.

"Well, we still have a family box at Oaklawn—the home of the Arkansas Derby," says Patrick in self-defense, "and corned beef is still at the top of my list. It's a perennial winner and makes a great show when you have the guys over. But before you get to make a corned beef sandwich, you have to cook the beef.

"I get it and its little package of spice at the local fancy market, boil it as long as it says to, and add cabbage, potatoes, and other vegetables toward the end. The meat shrinks and gives off a lot of fat. If it's winter—and winter is the time for corned beef, not summer—you can stick the pot in the snow when you're done cooking so that all the fat congeals. Then you can scrape it off. Now you can make the sandwich: slice the meat thinly across the grain, put it on rye, and add a lot of mustard and horseradish. Have the vegetables on the side. A slab of corned beef will make sandwiches for the better part of a week."

Of course, corned beef and cabbage is revisited every Saint Patrick's Day, but I've found a way to make

it less dreary if not actually uplifting and spring-like. It's simple. Use golden beets, baby bok choy, and radishes for the vegetable accompaniments; add the rosy slices of meat and it all looks like a spring garden. And the leftovers still make plenty of sandwiches.

Men, many of them, do like their meat. Among all the men we spoke with, just one suggested that he might use his solitary nights for the opportunity to have a salad for dinner. This was an amicable African American man I sat next to on a flight to Atlanta, who knew a thing or two about barbecue and a lot about cheesecake, his favorite food. Salad came in second. I ended up with a list of the best places to get cheesecake from New York to Atlanta, then over to Kentucky. But this man was actually passionate about salads, and I never would have pinned him for a salad man. He patted his ample front and said, "It's good that I love them. I need to eat salads!"

The publisher of one of America's more astute food journals mentioned that he eats meat six out of seven days a week. It might be a roast or the fattiest, thickest pork chop he can find, served with a baked potato—a weekend menu, he said. "I deglaze the pork chop with white wine and most of the time I overcook it because even though the danger of trichinosis is low—1 percent if the hog has been fed garbage, $\frac{1}{10}$ of a percent without the garbage—the problem is, you never know."

There's a pause, then he changes direction and remarks that because his schedule is the same weekday or weekend, he'll most likely cook a steak—logic that is lost on me.

"I like the raunchy chuck-end of a rib eye," he says, nearly smacking his lips. "I sauté it, or I should say 'fry' it, with a lot of fat. I put olive oil with the fat trimmings in a stainless steel skillet and fry it hot. Salt and pepper go on before, garlic after. I also take a piece of bread, toast it, rub it with garlic, and drizzle it with more oil."

In case you're wondering, this man is thin. Maybe because he tempers his excesses with a lettuce or arugula salad with freshly cut raw onions. Or maybe because he eats everything with red wine and ends his meal with a tiny piece of chocolate, which is no doubt beneficial if you're going to dig into the raunchy end of a rib eye a few times a week. And to think Patrick interviewed him years before we knew that red wine and chocolate were heart savers and all of that. A man ahead of his time.

A scholarly British author living in France told us that when he's batching it, he buys a piece of meat, usually a lamb chop. But this is no simple throw-it-in-the-pan-then-eat-it affair. "I look among the vegetables and pick something my wife doesn't like, like parsnips. She really dislikes parsnips. Then I look into the cupboard to see what appeals to me. I open a stout or a cold Pelforth Brune, and I also open a bottle of wine, for the cooking, you know. Chiles are going to be among the spices I'll use—fresh red chile, fresh ginger—the tingle-and-burn spices."

While I'm trying to grasp exactly where this is going, our acquaintance reveals that he is in possession of the most essential ingredient for all good cooks—a garden.

"Next," he continues, "I look out in the garden to see what's there. Sometimes we have wild sorrel, two or three kinds. If I'm lucky there will be horse mushrooms. But generally I want a bit more greenery, like cabbage. I chop it and eat it raw with a bit of olive oil and untoasted caraway seeds. I may put some of the seeds in the pan when I'm cooking the sorrel," he muses. "And I'll probably fry the

chop with some onion, then have more chopped onion on the side. The chile is going in the marinade, and some of it's going on the chop as I fry it."

We've lost track of the dish, but I think we've ended up with a **lamb chop with tingle-and-burn spices**, a dab of sorrel with caraway seeds, raw chopped onion, and some cabbage on the side. No parsnips, after all. Dessert, once he gets there, is ice cream with maple syrup. Whew!

We happen to know a few men who are both artists and ranchers, and a few others who combine writing and farming, difficult and generally low-margin careers, all, with few exceptions. One is artist-rancher James Turrell. James has been known to call himself a "light heavyweight." An artist who uses light as his medium, James injects light from lunar and solar sources into the interior of a spent volcanic cinder cone called Roden Crater. His cattle roam on thousands of dry-grass acres in the general vicinity of the crater, and artists from all over the world have made the pilgrimage to this extinct, bicolored volcano. When we stopped by to visit a few years ago, he served us

beef for dinner and beef for breakfast as well as lunch the next day. Ranchers' fare. I've learned through doing vegetarian cooking classes for the wives of Texas ranchers that the beef-beef-beef menu is not all that uncommon.

James's favorite beef dish is smoked beef with special sauce. "I resort to the smoking and basting thing," he confesses. "Fire up the smoker in the afternoon. Put on the meat. I like tenderloin. Flank and brisket I like as well, but tenderloin is all I eat. I'll have a salad with crumbled blue cheese. No potato. I stay away from the carbs. And no steak sauce compares with whiskey." And that's the special sauce. It can go on the meat or in the mouth. Or both.

Another rancher, Hugh Fitzsimmons—who is not an artist but who was once a high school history teacher—raises bison in south Texas. Hugh says, "When I eat alone I usually have a bison burger on an English muffin." That's not so surprising; he loves bison and he has a freezer full of it. But there's a trick to cooking it that Hugh has taught us.

"Go low and slow," he intones. "Don't hurry, and keep that heat turned way down." That way this very lean meat retains its tenderness. And that goes for all the other bison cuts he's been known to cook as well. (Incidentally, Hugh's bison isn't just any old buffalo. In 2007, Thunderheart Bison was the blue ribbon winner in the Gallo meat and charcuterie show in New York.)

Kaftes, or *keftes* (spellings vary by region), are basically meatballs wrapped around skewers and then grilled. Sari Abul-Jubein, the owner of Casablanca restaurant in Cambridge, Massachusetts, rustles up kaftes for his solitary meals. He seasons ground lamb with minced onion, cumin, allspice, chopped parsley, and pine nuts. They are really very good and not nearly as dense as other meat dishes.

"You make balls of the meat and squeeze the liquid out of them, skewer them, then put them on the grill," explains Sari. "They make a meal that's great to share with others or to enjoy alone. I have a salad with them, a tomato salad with onion, mint, olive oil, and lemon. Or a **yogurt salad with cucumber**, garlic, and mint."

This might well be the most wholesome of the men's meat meals we uncovered. The kaftes are smallish, the vegetables plentiful. True, planning might not be as crucial for Sari as it is for those who don't have a restaurant to raid. We imagine Sari strolling into Casablanca's kitchen, scooping up some seasoned lamb, grabbing a few tomatoes, then heading home to make or, rather, assemble his very appealing dinner. But then we made kaftes using some of Hugh's bison mixed with local lamb and found that it's an extremely straightforward dish. The salads are too, and together they make a great team for a hot-weather dinner. This is a menu we make often and eat with pleasure.

Meatballs, when you think about it, are close cousins to Sari's kaftes. As with kaftes, onion, herbs, and breadcrumbs are mixed with the meat, but meatballs are bigger and rounder, and are not on a stick. They're also more likely to be beef than lamb.

 Many a man's favorite pastime involves balls—football, basketball, baseball, and soccer. One year for the Super Bowl, Patrick fashioned an enormous pile of **meatballs** to serve his guests, along with a mountain of spaghetti. Architecturally, it makes more sense to serve meatballs with polenta than spaghetti. The competing shapes of spheres and lines just don't work well together, but it seemed easier to cook pasta and still keep an eye on the game. There were so many meatballs that we ended up freezing a dozen, which were much appreciated on snow-filled days when the roads were closed and there wasn't much to eat around the house. Without waiting for them to thaw, we cooked them slowly in a skillet where they defrosted and cooked simultaneously, much like the hamburger discussed below.

With cooking, planning is often a problem: predictably there will be hunger, but frequently there's no plan of attack. We don't think ahead, hence all this heat-and-serve food, takeout, cold cereal, and worse. Our instant-food, eat-and-go lifestyle provoked one television host to come up with a recipe based on the lack of planning—a rare and crispy burger that starts out with frozen hamburger that you forgot to defrost.

"You take a one-inch-thick frozen burger and put it in an un-oiled pan over low heat," he instructs. "The water from the thawing meat keeps it from sticking. Cook it like this for seven minutes on each side, then remove it from the skillet. Turn up the heat until the skillet is very hot, then put the burger back in and cook until it's crispy on each side."

This cook plops his burger on whole-wheat bread, adds ketchup and sliced sweet onions, salt and pepper. Sometimes he takes the bread and mops up the pan juices, something my father always did while my mother stood by, watching and appalled.

True, there are foods that men's wives will not eat, and many men will cook those foods when they find themselves alone, like the aforementioned parsnips. Blood sausage and tripe are other examples of man-alone foods. It's blood sausage that goes into one Englishman's spicy sausage, salad, and spuds, a rather better-than-usual version of bangers and mash, especially if you add the salad.

"Actually, I cook any kind of sausage or bacon or ham, or a pork chop," he admits, explaining that girls, his wife included in that category, don't like that much meat. "And I drink more red wine than I normally would when they're not around," he adds.

"Then I make a special spicy salad—an **all-herb salad** with a whole bunch of minced cilantro, chives, parsley, rocket, and mint with olive oil and a couple of drops of balsamic vinegar over the greens." This is a provocative salad because it's so familiar and exotic at the same time, so unexpectedly complex. A salad recipe is needed in this chapter, and a spicy herb salad goes well with meat, especially grilled meat.

Cookbook author Cliff Wright also goes for blood sausage when he eats alone—that and quite a few other things no one else will eat. It might be Polish-style blood sausage bought from a local Polish deli, with a fried egg on top. Or tripe in tomato sauce or a pan-seared Muscovy duck breast. "Others would like that, but I can't afford to buy more than one, so I usually have it when I'm alone. And my vegetables," Cliff adds, "are very simple, like broccoli and butter. And I mean, that's it."

But Cliff is no stranger to a steak. "I'll do a pan-seared **marinated tri-tip** soaked in a two-week-old not-so-great bottle of red wine that I couldn't bring myself to throw out," he says. "Gotta pat dry the steak before searing it, of course. I'll have it with spinach cooked in cream and with chive butter. I always make compound butters with leftover herbs. You know how you buy a little package of tarragon or chives, and then it just sits in the fridge? This way you extend its life."

How many of us have watched two dollars' worth of chives gradually yellow, then wither away just because we didn't get around to figuring out what to do with them beyond the dictates of a single recipe? What a waste! Especially when cooking for one. If you don't happen to have an herb garden—and most people don't, sad to say—fresh herbs other than parsley and cilantro can get pretty pricey. Herb butter lets you use every leaf and repays you with its flavor later. It will be used and loved. And it's not only good on the steak, but on potatoes, in soups, and with vegetables of all kinds.

Although simplicity is one of the advantages of choosing a steak, chop, or hamburger for dinner, some men go for more complex doings. John, the bartender at Lola's, a Cuban restaurant that enjoyed far too brief a stay in Santa Fe, inspired another meat dish. Over a mojito, Patrick extracted a recipe from him that is our most complicated one by far, but eminently doable and worth doing, though perhaps for a party rather than a meal alone, unless, like John, you plan to eat off of it all week. The recipe is for a stuffed, rolled flank steak, pierced with toothpicks or bound with twine, then grilled.

"I like my mother's cooking," John says. "She's Hungarian and my father's Italian. I always buy fresh and love to cook on the grill. When it comes to a flank steak, marinate it," he says. "Just use an Italian vinaigrette. Then make mushroom duxelles."

Responding to Patrick's blank look, he adds, "Basically, you take mushrooms and chop them up fine, squeeze all the water out, then sauté them in butter with scallions."

So far, so good.

"Then I grate Swiss cheese, crumble bacon, about eight strips, get parsley, and put it all in the center of the flank steak. You roll it up, wrap it like a football, put toothpicks through it, and grill."

He makes it sound easy, and it definitely sounds easier than his other favorite dish, another stuffed meat concoction, only this time one involving a chicken. It's an impressive one, and it's even more impressive to think that John would cook this just for himself. We suspect that he may not be telling the truth.

"Carefully strip all the skin off the chicken," he begins. "Take off all the meat. Throw away the bones and stuff the chicken meat in the Cuisinart. Add ham and pistachios and blend. Also buy two chicken breasts. Cut them into big pieces and throw them into the mix. Then put it all back in the chicken skin. Make a little sack out of it, take cheesecloth, soak it in melted butter, then wrap the whole thing up like an Italian cheese that looks like a pumpkin."

This required a napkin note, a diagram.

"Then you bake it until a meat thermometer reads 'chicken is done.'" And so are you, we imagine.

The director of his own theater company turns to jerked pork when he's on his own. "Marinate a pork tenderloin in jerk sauce from the store," John Flax says, "then grill it. You're supposed to serve it with plantains, but I eat it with baked acorn squash and greens, either collard, mustard, or beet greens, and sometimes a combo of all three."

This sounds like an eminently doable meal too, even with the plantains. But they could be the final straw for many a single man. Meat, greens, and squash are already an impressive showing.

Jerk sauce provides a solution for another man who douses chicken with it. "I'll marinate a bunch of **chicken breasts** in jarred jerk sauce, then pan-fry them in any oil," he says. "You make some rice along with it and the chicken goes on top of the rice. Add greens. Kale, collards, chard, mustard, beet greens, or broccoli raab," he suggests. "A green is a good thing."

Chicken soup almost skips the jerk sauce, but not the bird. Joe Simone says that when he's alone, he browns a whole chicken in oil, adds carrots, onion, celery, fennel, and whole sage leaves along with some mashed garlic and a squeeze of lemon. Then he adds chicken broth, covers the pot, and simmers until done. The chicken gets sliced, then served in a bowl with polenta. "This way you can make a chicken last for a couple of days," he explains.

Of course, any whole chicken will last a single eater for more than a few days, but with the broth and vegetables, this sounded like a particularly satisfying and unusually well-balanced meal. Once you've made it, the vegetables are there, waiting for you.

A few men mentioned cooking a tri-tip and having it around for a few days' worth of sandwiches, so we bought one from a local rancher and cooked it, following Cliff's lead of marinating it overnight in red wine. Others suggested using a flank steak instead. Either way, you'll want to slice it very thin, particularly if it's grass-fed beef, which tends to be extra lean and not as tender as grain-fed.

1 tri-tip, weighing
2 to 3 pounds
2 cups red wine
2 tablespoons olive oil
2 garlic cloves, sliced
salt and pepper
chive butter (page 122)

1. The night before you plan to cook it, cover the tri-tip with the wine, olive oil, garlic, and plenty of freshly ground pepper. Put it all in a zip-lock bag and refrigerate. When you think of it, squish it around in the bag so that all the meat is exposed to the marinade.

2. When you're ready to cook it, let the meat come to room temperature. Remove it from the marinade, set it on a few layers of paper towels, and blot with more paper towels, getting it as dry as you can.

3. Heat a cast-iron skillet over a high flame until very hot—you can tell when you place your hand over it; you'll feel a thick heat. Brush olive oil over the meat, season it well with salt and freshly ground pepper, then drape it into the skillet and sear on both sides just until brown. Reduce the heat to low. Cover the pan and cook until the internal temperature reads 125 degrees F, about 25 minutes for medium-rare. Remove to a plate and let rest for 10 minutes, then slice thinly across the grain. Have some warm for dinner, with chive butter melting over it, then use the rest for sandwiches.

CHIVE BUTTER (AND OTHER HERB BUTTERS)

One way to make chive butter is to purée the chives to make a butter that's green throughout. Another is to snip the chives, then cream them into the butter. Combine methods and you end up with a green butter flecked with chives. This is a very flexible sort of thing. It doesn't even have to be chives. Any other fresh herbs, really, will be good here too—parsley, marjoram, oregano, dill—alone or in combination.

1 bunch chives
1 stick butter, softened
grated zest of 1 lemon
a few pinches salt, to taste
white or black pepper

1. Thinly slice the chives and throw most of them into a bowl with the butter. Chop the remainder with a knife so that they break down, and add those to the butter as well. Mix the chives, butter, and lemon zest with a wooden spoon or your hands until well blended. Add a few pinches of salt and some freshly ground pepper.

2. Set aside any butter you plan to use right away, then scrape the rest of the butter onto a piece of wax paper and roughly shape it into a log. Wrap it up, then draw the log through your thumb and forefinger to stretch it into a uniform cylinder, and freeze until needed. Take it out and cut off rounds of butter to use at will.

> **WHERE TO USE CHIVE BUTTER**
>
> Cliff used his chive butter on steak, but all herb butters are good over fish and chicken, too. When it comes to the plant world, consider stirring a green-flecked round of butter into a potato soup, a bowl of polenta, a pot of rice, or putting it on a baked potato or a dish of lentils. As it melts, it seasons your dish and flecks it with bits of green. Once you have herb butter on hand, you'll find it provides instant enhancement of all kinds of warm foods.

An herb salad startles the tongue and makes a lively side to all kinds of foods, especially meats. Everything is torn rather than chopped. If you have an herb garden, don't hesitate to include herbs other than those mentioned here, such as sorrel, lemon thyme, marjoram, different kinds of basil, and chives.

1 handful small spinach leaves

1 handful cilantro leaves

1 handful any or all of the following herbs:

  Italian parsley

  arugula

  dill sprigs

  lovage or celery leaves

  small mint leaves, torn

2 scallions, including some of the greens

salt

1 tablespoon extra-virgin olive oil

1 teaspoon fresh lemon juice

Tear or cut the spinach and cilantro into bite-size pieces, pluck or tear the herbs, and slice the scallions. Toss all the greens together with a few pinches of salt, then drizzle with olive oil. Toss well to coat the leaves, then toss one more time with lemon juice. Taste and add more oil or lemon juice, if needed.

LAMB CHOPS WITH TINGLE-AND-BURN SPICES

To get the tingle-and-burn spices this solo eater was drawn to, we made a sauce of pure ground red chile, garlic, spices, and olive oil. It definitely added those elements.

THE LAMB	THE SAUCE
2 or 3 lamb chops	1 large garlic clove
salt and pepper	salt
ground cumin	1 scant tablespoon ground red chile
a few pinches of red pepper flakes	1/4 teaspoon each of ground cumin,
olive oil	coriander, and caraway
juice of 1/2 lemon	1 tablespoon olive oil

1. Rub the lamb chops with plenty of salt, freshly ground pepper, cumin, and red pepper flakes. Drizzle a little oil over the meat and then squeeze the lemon over all. Cover and refrigerate for at least an hour. Let the chops return to room temperature before cooking.

2. To make the sauce, smash the garlic in a mortar with a few pinches of salt to break it up. Add the chile and spices and work them into the garlic with the oil.

3. Grill your lamb chops on an outdoor gas or charcoal grill, or a ridged pan placed over high heat, for a few minutes on each side or until they're as done as you like them. Let them rest on a plate for several minutes, then spread the sauce over them. Serve with the spicy herb salad (page 123).

Here is our interpretation of Sari's lamb kaftes and cucumber-yogurt salad with mint, which we serve with bulgur or rice. Because one pound of lamb will make enough of these little sausage-shaped meats for four big eaters, a single eater might want to use only half that much. And if you don't want to eat them twice in a week, shape, then freeze the meat that you don't cook, and it will be there waiting for you.

¹/₂ pound ground lamb

1 slice bread

¹/₂ onion, grated

2 tablespoons chopped parsley

¹/₂ teaspoon black pepper

¹/₂ teaspoon ground cumin

¹/₂ teaspoon paprika

¹/₄ teaspoon allspice

¹/₂ teaspoon salt

Kaftes are absolutely delicious grilled over a wood fire, but if it's winter and snowing, or if you don't have a grill or want to light a fire for yourself, they can be cooked to good effect on a ridged cast-iron pan, which happens to leave nice-looking grill marks as a bonus.

1. Put the lamb in a bowl. Cover the bread with water and let it stand until soft while you grate the onion on the large holes of a standing grater. Add the onion to the lamb along with the parsley, spices, and salt. Squeeze the water out of the bread, add the bread to the bowl, and then mix everything together until the meat begins to develop some elasticity. You can do this in a mixer, or just get your hands in the bowl and knead the meat until you sense a change. Cover, refrigerate, and let rest for an hour for the seasonings to blend.

2. If you're going to grill the meat, fashion it into torpedo-shaped pieces, then stick your skewer right into the middle of each one and squeeze the meat around it. If using a pan, you won't need the skewers.

3. Cook the kaftes on the grill or in a hot lightly oiled pan, turning them as they color, until they feel firm and are beautifully browned on the outside, about 10 minutes, depending on how big they are. Serve with rice or bulgur, cucumber salad, or, as Sari suggests, a salad of sliced tomatoes with olive oil and mint.

CUCUMBER-YOGURT SALAD

Scaled back to make one generous serving, grated cucumber gives this dish an almost sauce-like texture. If you prefer more discrete elements, seed, then dice the cucumber instead. This is a refreshing salad to eat with all kinds of food, and it can appear as one of several salads in salad meals. In summer, it's practically thirst quenching.

1 garlic clove, not too large,
　coarsely chopped
¼ teaspoon salt
½ cup yogurt
1 cucumber, peeled
3 pinches dried mint leaves or
　2 mint leaves, finely chopped
olive oil

1. Smash the garlic in a mortar with the salt until it's smooth, then stir in the yogurt.

2. Grate the cucumber on the large holes of a standing grater, stopping when you get to the seeded middle part. Discard that. Squeeze what will be a considerable amount of moisture out of the cucumber, then mix the cucumber with the yogurt. Put it in a dish, garnish with the mint, and drizzle just a little olive oil over the surface.

Like kaftes, meatballs are made with ground meat mixed with breadcrumbs, onion, and various seasonings. But they're round, browned, then simmered in tomato sauce rather than grilled. They freeze well and can be reheated as needed, which, in the eyes of some, makes them a perfect bachelor food. Patrick makes them extra-large, while Peggy Markel, a cook who leads cooking tours, makes her spicy Moroccan meatballs about the size of big marbles. One could do the same with these, or go for an in between size. We use local grass-fed beef, bison, or a mixture—very lean but flavorful meats.

1 pound ground beef or bison

a handful of parsley leaves, finely chopped with 1 large garlic clove

1 small onion, finely diced

1/2 cup breadcrumbs, fresh or dried

1/2 teaspoon dried oregano

1 egg

1/2 cup (or more if meat is very lean) grated Asiago or other grating cheese

salt and pepper

2 tablespoons olive oil

tomato sauce (page 230)

1. Crumble the beef into a bowl, then add the chopped parsley, onion, breadcrumbs, oregano, egg, and cheese. Mix with your hands. Season with 1/2 teaspoon salt and freshly ground pepper, and mix again. Fry a little bit of the meat, then taste it to see if you've got the seasonings right; add more if needed.

2. Shape the meat into balls with your hands, making them as large or as small as you wish. Two- or three-inch balls seem like good sizes— substantial, but not too large.

3. Heat the oil in a skillet over medium heat if using grass-fed beef or bison, slightly higher heat if using fattier meat. When hot, add the meatballs and brown them, turning them so that they color more or less evenly.

4. Bring the tomato sauce to a simmer in a wide skillet. Add the meatballs and simmer gently until they're cooked through, about 20 minutes depending on the size. Serve with polenta or spaghetti.

BARTENDER'S FLANK STEAK STUFFED WITH MUSHROOMS AND MORE

Flank steak may be familiar fare for many, but it was unknown to us until we made this dish suggested by Lola's savvy bartender. A few things to note. First, it's really good. Second, a 1½-pound steak served five women and one man, so as a solo dish, you'd probably want to cut this back to a pound. Third, it's obvious that having beef with bacon and cheese flies in the face of a number of culinary and dietary no-no's. However, we did cut way back on the offending additions, leaving just enough for great taste. While spinach wasn't mentioned as one of the fillings, it is good here. We recommend cooking a large bunch of spinach, chopping it up, and sprinkling it over the meat before adding the mushrooms.

1 to 1½ pounds flank steak
juice of 1 large lemon, about
   3 tablespoons
salt and pepper
½ pound crimini mushrooms or other
   fresh mushrooms
olive oil, as needed
1 shallot, finely diced
1 tablespoon chopped parsley
3 pieces thin or 2 pieces thick bacon
1 large bunch spinach, stems removed
   and leaves washed but not dried
1 cup grated Gruyère or Jarlsburg cheese

1. Ask your butcher to run the steak through a tenderizer. It really does make it tender, even if it looks a little lacy. Though now not necessary, you can still put the perforated meat in a dish with the fresh lemon juice, salt, and freshly ground pepper, and set it aside while you get all the fillings together. (If the meat wasn't tenderized, a stay of an hour or more in the marinade is needed to help make the meat tender.)

2. Rinse the mushrooms quickly in a bowl of water, then pulse them 6 or 7 times in a food processor to break them up so that they're finely chopped. Heat the oil in a wide skillet, add the mushrooms and shallot, and cook over high heat, stirring often, until the mushrooms have released most of their liquid, after about 8 to 10 minutes. Stir in the parsley and season with salt and pepper to taste.

3. Fry the bacon until crisp, then crumble up thin pieces or, if thick, chop it. Wilt the spinach in a wide skillet until it's tender and bright green, after just a few minutes. Put it in a strainer and press out as much liquid as you can, then chop it coarsely.

4. To assemble the dish, lay the steak on a work surface. Season with salt and freshly ground pepper if it hasn't been seasoned already. Spread the mushrooms over the meat, followed by the bacon, spinach, and finally, the cheese. Roll it up and tie with kitchen string to keep the fillings intact, or skewer with toothpicks. Refrigerate until an hour before you are ready to grill, bringing it to room temperature before grilling.

5. To cook, preheat a gas grill on high until hot. Brush the meat with olive oil, then put on the grill, turning it every few minutes until the whole surface has been seared. Reduce the heat to medium and cook for 20 minutes if the meat was put through a tenderizer, up to 30 minutes if it wasn't, or until a meat thermometer reads 125 degrees F. Remove to a platter, cover loosely with foil, and let rest for 10 minutes before snipping the string and slicing the meat into rounds.

Why almost? Because the point wasn't to make enough broth for a soup, but to end up with a sauce to moisten the chicken and vegetables. This is a straightforward, practical, and rather comforting dish you can eat from for days—and not always in the same way. But choose a small bird so that you don't get tired of it. Three pounds is plenty. This is a somewhat improvisational dish, so you can use different vegetables and more or less of them. You can also use chicken parts rather than a whole bird; and if you're not one to eat off a dish for days, you can simply make a smaller version.

1 whole small chicken or
  6 chicken parts
salt and pepper
olive oil for frying and finishing
4 to 6 medium-size carrots, peeled
1 fennel bulb, or 1 celery heart,
  quartered
1 large onion, root end intact,
  halved and quartered
5 garlic cloves, peeled
1 bay leaf
2 pinches dried thyme
1 lemon, quartered
2 cups chicken stock
soft polenta (page 64)
chopped parsley, marjoram, or
  oregano to finish

1. Rinse, then pat dry the chicken and season it with salt and freshly ground pepper. Heat a few tablespoons olive oil in a deep pot, such as a Dutch oven, and brown the chicken over medium heat until golden. Since this will take about 15 minutes, you'll have plenty of time to peel carrots, quarter the fennel and onion, and peel the garlic.

2. Tuck the vegetables, garlic, bay leaf, thyme, and lemon quarters around the chicken, then pour in the chicken stock. (It will not cover the bird, but if you cover the pot, it won't dry out.) Bring just to a boil, then lower the heat, cover the pot, and cook gently until the chicken is done, about an hour for whole, less for parts.

3. To serve, spoon warm polenta into a wide, shallow pasta plate or soup bowl. If you cooked a whole chicken, carve off whatever parts you wish to eat and lay them around the polenta along with some of the vegetables. Spoon broth around all, drizzle olive oil over the top, and add a sprinkling of herbs and plenty of freshly ground pepper.

THREE OR FOUR WAYS TO EAT CHICKEN SOUP ALMOST

Because the vegetables will soften and become less appealing once they're reheated, enjoy them the first one or two times you eat the dish. After that, serve the chicken over rice and flavor the broth with a pinch of cumin, minced jalapeño, and cilantro. Finally, use the moist meat for sandwiches or a chicken salad, and use any extra broth to enhance a soup or risotto.

We were long in coming to jerk sauce, but having made it, we fully appreciate why some of our solo eaters described what sounded like enormous mounds of jerked chicken for their eat-alone foods. It's that good. Still, it's a lot of food. But because grilled, jerked meats are good party food—you *want* to share the whole hot, sticky experience with others—we suspect these men are entertaining.

There are a million jarred jerk sauces—just look on the Internet. But we suggest making your own, because it's an amazing thing to work with all the pungent spices and searing chiles.

1 small onion, roughly chopped

4 scallions, chopped

3 garlic cloves, peeled

2 habanero peppers, quartered

1 tablespoon brown sugar

1 teaspoon ground allspice

1 teaspoon ground black pepper

1/2 teaspoon ground nutmeg

1/4 teaspoon ground cinnamon

2 teaspoons salt

3 tablespoons fresh lime juice

1 1/2 tablespoons soy sauce

3 tablespoons olive or canola oil

3 pounds chicken, cut up

Serve with the steamed kale with sesame oil and rice wine vinegar, brown or white rice (pages 222 and 223), and black-eyed peas. The wine jelly (page 262) makes a much-needed cooling dessert.

1. Put all the ingredients except the chicken in a blender or food processor and purée until smooth. Pour it over the chicken pieces, put them in a ziplock plastic bag, and squish it around so that everything is in contact with the marinade. Refrigerate overnight or over the course of a day, occasionally turning the meat.

2. When ready to cook, let the chicken come to room temperature for an hour.

3. If grilling, which is ideal, make a wood fire or charcoal fire and wait until the coals are ash-covered and the heat is no longer super hot. Or heat a gas grill. Brush your clean grill with oil because the sauce tends to stick, then grill the chicken, skin side down first so that it gets a nice crust. Turn to brown on both sides. (You might want to subdue flare-ups with a mist of water.) Once browned, move the chicken to a cooler part of the grill, cover, and cook until done, about 30 minutes or more, if the coals have started to cool off. (Large legs might take longer, if you've included them; wings less.)

4. To bake the chicken, which is also very good but minus the wood smoke, heat the oven to 400 degrees F. Lay the chicken pieces in one or two shallow dishes in a single layer, and bake, turning once, until crusty and browned, about 45 minutes.

How to Eat Alone

While it's still light out
set the table for one:
a red-linen table cloth,
one white plate, a bowl
for the salad
and the proper silverware.
Take out a three-pound leg of lamb,
rub it with salt, pepper and cumin,
then push in two cloves
of garlic splinters.
Place it in a 325-degree oven
and set the timer for an hour.
Put freshly cut vegetables
into a pot with some herbs
and the crudest olive oil
you can find.
Heat on a low flame.
Clean the salad.
Be sure the dressing is made
with fresh dill, mustard
and the juice of hard lemons.

Open a bottle of good three-year-old zinfandel
and let it breathe on the table.
Pour yourself a glass
of cold California chardonnay
and go to your study and read.
As the story unfolds
you will smell the lamb
and the vegetables.
This is the best part of the evening:
the food cooking, the armchair,
the book and bright flavor
of the chilled wine.
When the timer goes off
toss the salad
and prepare the vegetables
and the lamb. Bring them out
to the table. Light the candles
and pour the red wine
into your glass.
Before you begin to eat,
raise your glass in honor
of yourself.
The company is the best you'll ever have.

—Daniel Halpern

CHAPTER 7

Alone at Last

"Basically, it's about comforting carbs and good salt."
—Amelia Saltsman, *cook and food writer*

WOMEN (AND SOME MEN) WHO ARE TIRED of cooking for those ingrates called children and the occasional spouse, who are weary of cleaning up after meals and bored with eating on a schedule that says it's dinnertime when really it's time for something else, know the pleasure of being alone at last in one's kitchen. It's an enjoyable moment when we get to eat whatever and whenever we want—and wherever, too, for that matter.

Like staring into a closet filled with clothes and finding nothing to wear, sometimes we gaze into our refrigerators and whether they're double Sub-Zeros or tiny under-the-counter numbers, we find nothing to eat. Sometimes there *is* nothing to eat. I have seen women's refrigerators with little more than bottles of water, some cartons of restaurant remains, and ice cream in the freezer. Others may have food in them, but it can appear useless unless, of course, we have the eye to pick out those bits and pieces that can eventually become a frittata, a salad, or a more-than-decent sandwich. After all, we do need to feed ourselves something more substantial, not to mention ceremonial, than Sad Girl's Macaroni and Cheese, which, I've recently been told, consists of boiled spaghetti with pregrated Parm sprinkled on top. At the very least, it helps to be ready for those times we're alone with a modestly well-stocked refrigerator and cupboard, that at least contain eggs, some canned tomatoes, bread or cereal, perhaps, and a few good vegetables.

When it comes to the rare night alone, women can get pretty basic and simply go for the leftovers. Says one food writer, "I often make a salad and just throw in whatever form of protein I'm having. And if I have a pot of soup or stew hanging around, I'll have that, and that's just fine."

But there are those who disdain leftovers, thus depriving themselves of that time-honored meal option. They will never take the uneaten half of their meal home from a restaurant, nor stash that bit of whatever remains from dinner into a container for later. This means that each time they want to eat, they have to start from scratch.

Some women simply dislike the challenge of cooking for themselves. "How am I going to cut up half a carrot?" one asks me, her voice practically caustic with frustration at something so unreasonable as this. "And what am I supposed to do with the other half?"

Sometimes the no-leftovers and don't-like-to-cook-for-one people are the same. If you're in the camp that likes leftovers, you'll probably just cut up the whole carrot, eat half, and worry no more. These are questions that those of us who are leftover eaters can't imagine asking, but they are vivid and troubling for others.

Sandwiches were the solution to this set of problems for one woman—not making them, mind you, but going to the deli and getting either a half if she has just a normal appetite, or, if she's really hungry, a whole sandwich to take home. Here was a parcel of food she could enjoy by herself without fear of leftovers.

Some women admit that when they are finally alone they revert to those personal foods that are too odd to share—the cookie dough, the saltines crushed into a glass of milk. "It's comforting," says the author of that last idea, and when comfort is needed, women don't mind admitting it. Others might turn to the infamous bowl of cereal or microwaved popcorn for dinner. Relying on such insta-foods, cobbling dinner out of leftovers, or dining on a piece of toast smeared with peanut butter doesn't necessarily mean that we don't care for ourselves. Rather, it suggests that we're on vacation from routine and taking a break from caring for others. And, in fact, popcorn can be pretty good. Butter and sea salt are great on it, but what about truffle oil? Olive oil and smoked paprika? Or the fabulous Indian-spiced popcorn of Chef Floyd Cardoz? (And you don't need a microwave to make popcorn. It's actually quite fun to pop your own in a skillet, listening to the kernels ping against the lid and guessing if they'll all be popped when you finally dare to look.)

Writer Fran McCullough, who has no end of menu options up her sleeve having worked with many cookbook writers, knows just what she'll eat when she's alone at last. "I'll have my favorite Paris lunch— smoked salmon on a slice of buttered sourdough bread with sliced onion, capers, and a squeeze of lemon." And what could be easier to make for oneself? A Paris lunch sounds far more respectable than take-out, and yet it's certainly quicker than other shortcut foods, like mac and cheese. And when you arrange your Paris lunch on your favorite plate and sit down to enjoy it, you know that you are treating yourself well.

Amanda Archibald, who is French and English, which might explain why she is so civilized, expresses what I think of as the feminine ideal of solo eating. "Being alone or among people does not change what I eat," Amanda says. And this is unusual. "I may stand at the counter in my kitchen, especially during aperitif time or while preparing dinner, but then, I sit down to eat. Always. And I have no food secrets like chocolate hoarding."

Amanda will have cooked her dinner using vegetables from her CSA box, delivered from a nearby farm; it will probably include a special cheese; and she will have opened a bottle of wine to enjoy with her meal. Many women enjoy having something to drink with their solitary dinners.

"I'll open a nice bottle when he's gone," says Melissa, a magazine editor, "but I won't spend much time cooking since I do that when he's here."

"I have a kir while I'm preparing dinner," says writer Sylvia Thompson, "then a glass of wine with my meal."

"I'll have wine *if* some is open," adds Maureen Stein.

In defense of chocolate hoarding, I have to refer to Joanne Neft, who admits with no shame whatsoever that she hides a box of See's caramels with walnuts in a secret place. She says, "I can make a one-pound box last three months or longer. There's something about the safety of knowing where I squirreled it away and that it's there to satisfy my sweet tooth when I need it."

But when it comes to solitary meals, chocolate isn't necessarily on Joanne's menu. Thrilled to find herself home alone, she says, "I love it when he's gone. It's quiet and the house tends to be less messy. I can go to bed at 6:30 or wait until 11:00. I can sit in a bubble bath and read for two hours. I play my opera music very loud. I get on the phone with a friend or two and we talk for many minutes. And, I tend to get in a bread-making mood. Funny, isn't it?"

And this is when she takes the opportunity to cook some of her favorite foods, like pickled herring and caramelized onions over mashed potatoes.

"So the truth will be out," Joanne confesses, "when no one is looking (and no one is around to complain), I buy a large jar of pickled herring (not the kind rolling around in sour cream), boil enough potatoes for mashing with either cream or good butter, and while the potatoes are cooking, I caramelize some sweet onions, then top the potatoes with them and a good portion of herring. It's a silly German thing."

Just when I have decided I want to give this dish a try, Joanne adds, "Now that I think about it, it doesn't sound too appetizing, does it? But it works for the 100 percent German in me."

The dish is good. And it's pretty, too, with the blue-skinned slices of herring snuggling among the golden onions, a spoonful of sour cream melting down the potatoes.

A young writer named Rae Paris says Tater Tots were once her secret eat-alone food. "But they're not necessarily an eat-alone food anymore," she says. "My husband and I have been together for long enough that I've stopped caring if he's around when I eat them. And now he likes them, too. But I've gone back to eating them when I'm alone and he's gone, so I can have them to myself. I can't believe that I've become territorial about Tater Tots!" she says. "Tater Tots

with ketchup. They remind me of elementary school—fourth grade, crushes, lunch lines, that oddly warm and comforting strange cafeteria smell—like wet concrete after a warm Los Angeles rain."

My sister has discovered, as have others, that being home alone and not having to cook or clean up for anyone but herself means that time expands. Here's the strategy she used for a week alone last summer. "For dinner I made an omelet, picked tomatoes from the garden, sliced them, and put pepper on them. I drank water or a gin and tonic. I had a few almonds. And with all the time I saved? I cleaned out my closet, including all the nooks and crannies. Then I cleaned out all the cupboards in the kitchen. I cleaned out the bookshelf in my office. I bought curtains and put them up in the bedroom—I've been promising for three years to do that—and I talked to a consultant about converting to solar heat. I walked the dog every day. Twice. And I read."

Despite the pleasures and gains that can be reaped by being alone at home, not every woman is delighted about those times when she's in her house without her family. "Frankly, I try never to eat alone," says ceramicist Sandy Simon, who, on a normal day, would be cooking for her husband and one or two of her kids. "It's lonely, but I'd never eat out alone—that's *really* lonely. So I eat in my house. Probably some shrimp or a steak. And a salad." Then she adds, "I do eat less if I'm alone, though."

Like Sandy, I don't enjoy eating alone that much, either, although I never mind it in a restaurant. So the two nights each week that Patrick stays at his studio, I invariably invite a friend over, eat with a neighbor, or I skip. Sometimes it feels good to just not eat anything at all. Days alone can be good for fasting, if you're inclined to do that.

The simple, oval egg, in a variety of forms, is the choice for many women. Eggs manage to be comforting, nutritious, and quick to prepare. "Eggs are my go-to food when I'm alone," a woman in a workshop confides. "My favorite pan is a small cast-iron skillet that was my grandmother's. It holds just one egg."

"Eggs," declares Fran McCullough, having given the question more thought. "My favorite is **Judy's eggs with crunchy breadcrumbs**, which is kind of elegant in a very humble way."

Adding buttery crisp breadcrumbs to your eggs lifts them from the ordinary but without straying from the basic ingredients. It's only the form that changes, but that changes everything. Converting a slab of bread into rough little crumbs and then getting them crisp and delicious takes that tiny bit of extra care that transforms the ordinary into something that is, as Fran says, "kind of elegant." Add some asparagus and a glass of Sancerre and you have a fine little supper for any night of the week, one you could even share with others.

As powerful attractors for all kinds of fillings, frittatas and flat omelets are also a good way for the solo eater to go. You can fill them with ricotta cheese or leftover spaghetti, or you can make them with something fresh—sautéed spinach, mushrooms, caramelized onions, or asparagus. Frittatas are more substantial than an omelet and grander than a boiled egg, yet they're not any heavier or even much more trouble, especially if you enjoy slowing down at the end of the day to slice a few vegetables and chop a few herbs. In the end, frittatas feel more like a meal, more like dinner. And you might even end up with leftovers for lunch the next day.

Kim Carlson, publisher of the webzine *Culinate*, doesn't get to eat alone very often. "Not yet," she says, thinking of a time when her children will be grown. But one day she found herself home alone. "I cut up chunks of good whole wheat sourdough and browned them in a little olive oil in a sauté pan. Then I poached an egg. The croutons went into a bowl and the egg went on top with a little salt. It wasn't ambitious, but it was memorable! Was it because I was alone?" Kim mused, "Or because I actually cooked just for myself?"

When asked what she cooked when home alone, Emily Hartzog, a lithe surgeon who has spent a fair amount of time in England, said, "A hard-boiled egg sandwich," and left it at that. When asked to elaborate, she explained, "You have to gob on the mayo, slice the eggs very thin, salt and pepper generously, and add translucent slices of tomato. They sell these on the trains in England; it's practically the pinnacle of their cuisine." It could be (if done with good quality everything—eggs, tomatoes, bread, and mayonnaise) quite a fine sandwich.

"Scrambies," says cookbook author Martha Rose Shulman, but she doesn't mean the kind of scrambled eggs that are hastily done in a minute or less. Rather she's thinking about eggs that are creamy-smooth because they're cooked very, very slowly over a tiny flame. "But if Liam is there," (Liam is Martha's son) "the scrambled eggs get cooked faster over higher heat since he hasn't the patience or interest to wait for slowly cooked ones." Compromise is just what happens when another comes to the table.

Kate Manchester, publisher of *Edible Santa Fe,* takes up the theme of compromise. "Eating alone is nothing less than a luxurious, even decadent, act," she says, "because I get to think about myself. I don't have to think about someone else." And when the opportunity arrives, she tends to return to her past, which involves seafood since she's from Rhode Island. "I find myself searching for that connection," she says. But because good fish isn't always an option in New Mexico, she has a back-up menu. "If it isn't seafood, I'll make **johnny cakes** and eat them with syrup and butter. I'd never even think of making them for my boyfriend or eating them when he's here," she reflects. "It's a stolen moment when I can cook for my own palate."

The one-unit meal, like johnny cakes, sidesteps the notion of a square meal with several foods skillfully balancing one another. Food writer Amelia Saltsman, who has no end of beautiful foods available to her from the Santa Monica farmers market, says that, in the end, she may just have a baked potato with butter and salt. "Basically, it's about comforting carbs and good salt," she says.

Other such ultra-simple meals mentioned include a baked **sweet potato with goat cheese**; rye toast buttered and then rubbed with garlic; polenta; or a solitary vegetable—an entire cauliflower, a big artichoke, pounds of asparagus, or potatoes. An authority on Greek food and the author of gorgeous books on the same, Aglaia Kremezi says, "My dish is **fried potatoes with yogurt sauce**—thinly sliced potatoes, *lots* of them, but not sliced too thin, not like chips. I fry them in olive oil until soft and only slightly crunchy, and eat them with a sauce made of yogurt, crumbled feta, and mustard. It's no big deal, but it is really delicious and part of my solo ritual. I eat at the table, with a glass of wine, of course."

Knowing Aglaia's food firsthand and how good it is, we tried these potatoes and liked them a lot. They are the ultimate in indulgent oily little dishes. And the sauce was good on everything we could find to put it on. But because we weren't sure exactly what she had in mind, we asked for more specifics. Mustard, it turns out, was crucial. "Add enough so that it's not a very pretty color," she said, and that made the difference.

People told us, though not nearly as often as we would have expected, that when left alone in their own kitchens, they resorted to eating cereal for dinner. A little cloud of shame seems to hover around the cereal eaters, as if they know they really could do better and perhaps should try. One describes mixing different dried cereals together for dinner, a habit to which her whole extended family is committed. A man confesses to eating Life Cereal with Coffee-Mate. But the cereal supper isn't always about convenience, exhaustion, or lack of imagination. And the cereal isn't always cold. "When I'm home alone," writes a friend, "the thing I like most is that the moment is different from the normal routine of planning and preparing dinner for family or friends. So I often have breakfast for dinner—a bowl of steel-cut oats. I mean, who says why certain grains are for breakfast and others are for dinner? And in the evening I can linger over my 'breakfast' instead of hurrying off to start the day."

Who says, indeed? Breakfast for dinner, and we're back to eggs, a favorite and for good reason. "Eggs are simple, warm, and fairly quick," says peach farmer and writer Mas Masamoto. "But they have another function, too. As breakfast foods, they signal the start of something, even if it is mid-morning or the end of the day. I usually write in the very early morning—that's my first day. Then I work outside—that's my second day. But when I'm by myself, I start my third day with an omelet dinner, then retire to my desk and start writing again."

The solo meal we work into our lives, especially if we're busy with careers and small children, might be something we cobble together once, then go back to again and again. A young woman who's busy working as a caterer and raising a family always turns to a concoction she calls her fake Thai wrap.

"For this," she says, after apologizing that it's not real Thai, "you take peanut butter and spread it over a tortilla, add a big squirt of *sriracha* sauce, lettuce, bean sprouts, and pile on sliced carrots, basil, and mint." Hearing this, another woman, whose children are grown, added that her mother always made what she called a Texas summer sandwich, consisting of peanut butter, mayonnaise, tomatoes, cucumbers, and lettuce on bread. Both these sounded strange to me, but when I cast them as a kind of Thai salad with thick peanut sauce that happens to be served with tortillas or bread instead of a rice paper wrap or slippery noodles, they seemed more plausible. The mayonnaise might be problematic for some, though. Does it really belong with peanut butter? Some say "yes!" My high school French teacher thought it did, on something he called a hotsy-totsy bilala, essentially a peanut butter and mayonnaise sandwich. Now that I think about it, this must have been his eat-alone food.

You might assume that women are big salad eaters when they're alone, and some are. Maureen Callahan makes, and has shared, a beautiful summer salad of **bulgur with tomatoes and shrimp**; another woman forages in her garden for lettuce, cabbage, mint, purslane, and sorrel, then takes her salad meal to her balcony. Martha Rose, as might be expected for a vegetable-oriented cook, tends to make herself a salad when she gets to eat alone. "But a really nice salad," she insists, "with endives, a coddled egg, feta, herbs. If I have mushrooms or beets, I add them, too. Or walnuts. Or pine nuts."

But salads aren't for everyone. One woman confesses that she avoids having salads, even if they are healthy. Why? "I dislike making salads!" she says. "All that chopping and mixing and then having to craft a dressing; it's way too much work! For batch days, I go to a sandwich. There's something supremely satisfying about eating bread. If I can slather onto two slices of bread a great spread—like a roasted pepper–sun-dried tomato–cream cheese spread—and then pile on the veggies, sliced chicken or turkey, and finish it off with tons of lettuce, well, that's a hugely satisfying meal." It sounds a little like a salad to me, only stuffed between slices of bread.

Consider sentiment as something that drives a solo menu—cooking in a grandmother's skillet or making a grandmother's recipe. "After I first left home," says Marsha Weiner, "I found myself seeking time alone to make the dinner I had every Tuesday at my grandmother's house—salmon cakes, egg noodles with sour cream, and a wedge of iceberg lettuce with Russian dressing—you know, the mayonnaise, ketchup, and lemon stuff. I vividly recall my grandmother serving this on the dishes that came from the box of DUZ detergent, a white plate with a black rim and a red rosebud right in the middle. This was for me, then, pure comfort food," she recalls. "But now, if my husband is gone, I'll make myself things that we don't enjoy together, like fish or pasta. Usually I'll rent a favorite movie. But the salmon cake, noodles, and iceberg salad have been known to make an appearance even now."

As with men, women will cook things when they're alone that their husbands don't like. "Kidneys!" whispers Martha Rose, imitating her stepmother's breathless excitement at the thought of indulging in a favorite food disliked by her husband. "When Max goes out, I make myself kidneys!"

And then, there's the repetitive menu. Nancy Coonridge, who produces a fine goat cheese near Pie Town, New Mexico, says, "When I'm alone I eat organic chevron (goat meat), ground and topped with my organic goat cheese. I have that with a big glass of my organic raw goat milk. If my gardens are producing, I might have a salad with lettuce. Gee, if I could just grow a decent tomato, I would always have the perfect meal on hand."

This triple goat menu punctuated with salad is not that strange to those who raise food for a living. Mas Masamoto, on occasion, has also eaten from a limited menu based on what he grows, namely peaches and raisins. "Some of my worst habits come when I'm alone," he confesses, "and I slip into a creative mode, abusing myself by eating as a second act. I've had peach dinners some nights. That's it, just peaches. Grapes when in season with a dessert of raisins. Sometimes I'll add variety and eat apples and peaches and raisins. I've gotten some fairly intense stomachaches with all-fruit meals. But what's better than eating your own homegrown food?" Mas ponders before adding, "I suppose it would be healthier if I grew more variety on the farm."

And finally, there are those who turn to vegetables when dining alone. Many years ago an Australian friend told me the dish she made when she was at last home alone was canned tomatoes stewed in a little cream and spooned over toast. She said that it provided a soothing kind of nourishment. At the time I thought it was some odd Australian thing, but others have brought up stewed tomatoes as well.

If you squint, it is just a few steps away from *papa al pomodoro* and even closer perhaps to those wonderful soft, sweet tomato-and-bread pudding casseroles you find in cafeterias in the South.

Rosalind Cummins, a woman who, among other things, has made a solar gingerbread house, goes for **tomatoes on toast** for dinner. "Tomatoes sautéed in butter and served on toast with basil," she says. "Really, anything with tomatoes. And **mushrooms on toast** are good too." After Roz brought up tomatoes on toast, I gave them a try and now they've become my solo lunchtime staple—so easy, and warm in winter too.

When Roz was growing up, her family ate mushrooms on toast with a little bit of sherry on top. "I didn't know that other families didn't all have 'sherry shakers' on the table," she recalls. "I distinguished myself by asking for some sherry for my mushrooms at a friend's house. I guess I was destined to become a food writer."

Vegetables on toast, or supper sandwiches, as I call them, are one of my favorite solo dinners when I do cook. Basically, these are larger than usual bruschetta. Like Roz, I'm happy with just about any braised or sautéed vegetable piled over toast that's been brushed with olive oil and rubbed with garlic. The final touch is a shaving of cheese—a nice young or aged Asiago, a goat Gouda, or, in truth, whatever cheese happens to be around. The cheese melts into the vegetables and gives them that extra punch of flavor. It's a sandwich, in that bread is involved, but it's also a knife-and-fork food, which makes it that much more civilized, more of a sit-down meal.

While women, more often then men, find being in their kitchens when their families are away an experience that comes with a measure of relief, roles can be reversed. Take Pete Jensen, for example. "I can't believe you just asked me that!" he exclaimed when I asked the eating-alone question. "I just spent a week alone when my wife went off on a trip with a girlfriend. Mostly I do the cooking, yet I was stunned to find myself alone in the kitchen."

The reason Pete does most of the cooking is "because my wife works harder than I do and, like a typical man, I was looking for ways to show her I loved her." (Should all men be so typical!)

Even though he normally does all the cooking, the week of solitary dining had held some surprises for Pete. "I noticed that I got a lot more pleasure out of cooking for myself because I only had myself to think about for the first time in ages. I've been married thirty-seven years, and my wife's tastes are different than mine, so I know that to a certain degree cooking is about compromise. Suddenly, it was all about me! Cooking for myself was a pleasure.

"One night I had lamb chops—just rubbed them with salt and pepper and set them aside. I had time to make a mesquite fire. I absolutely love starting fires and tending them. It was as if I had my own little campfire in the backyard. I grilled up some zucchini, a little asparagus, some red onions with olive oil on them, and Spike. I'm addicted to Spike, like the spice hunters in *Dune*. It's probably something Gaylord Hauser put in it, I don't know, but I'm an addict!" Pete's thoughts trail off into the land of Spike, then return.

"Usually when I cook something simple, like boiled red potatoes," he says, "I make a few pounds of them because they're good for leftovers. But this time I made only three little potatoes and steamed them for myself. It was a ritual to choose three perfect potatoes and there were no leftovers because I was focused on making just enough for my meal. I really don't like leftovers, except for something that's naturally better the next day, like a curry or a stew. For the most part I'd rather have it alive and cooking."

Another thing that happened to Pete was that he noted the house was quiet. "I heard the sounds of my spoon tapping the edge of the bowl, the sound of water boiling. I enjoyed that a great deal. I plant milkweed every year for the Monarch butterflies, and I stood there and watched them feeding. Normally there'd be talk. There'd be friends—we entertain a lot—or my wife and I talk while we're cooking. The quiet was nice. It was good to eat alone."

We made Aglaia's eat–alone dish and loved it. But then, who wouldn't go for a dish of fried potatoes dipped in a tangy, mustardy yogurt sauce? Being an obliging cook, Aglaia says that you don't have to use as much oil as she does, that it needn't be all olive oil, and that you can slice your potatoes thicker if you like. Here's the recipe, in Aglaia's words.

potatoes, as many as you want to eat in a sitting, any kind

olive oil or sunflower seed oil

½ cup yogurt, preferably full-fat sheep's milk or cow's milk

2 tablespoons crumbled feta cheese, Greek, of course

2 to 3 teaspoons Dijon mustard, enough for an unattractive yellow shade

plenty of pepper or red pepper flakes

The Potatoes: "I halve my potatoes lengthwise, then slice them slightly thinner than ⅛ inch. Fry them in 2 inches of olive oil or half olive oil and half sunflower oil, or less. I don't like to let them get too golden, and I let only about half of them get crunchy. I drain them on three layers of paper towels."

The Sauce: "The so-called Greek yogurt you get is not the best kind for this. Basically very few of these thick yogurts are made with the traditional culture. I use regular cow or preferably sheep or goat's milk yogurt—the sourness compensates for the sweet-and-oily potatoes. Combine the yogurt, feta, mustard, and quite a bit of ground pepper or Aleppo pepper flakes. I once added some lemon zest, which you may or may not like. Help yourself to a few potatoes, take some sauce on the side, and dip each bunch of forked potatoes in the sauce and eat them."

Being a native Rhode Islander, Kate knows that a proper johnny cake has to be made with the proper grits, such as those made from Rhode Island White Cap flint corn. She further specifies Kenyon's johnny cake meal (www.kenyon gristmill.com) and says that you can use their white or yellow. There seem to be lots of debates over johnny cakes, from the spelling (with or without an "h"), to whether milk or water is used for the liquid, or both. Here is Kate's version.

1 cup Kenyon's johnny cake
   corn meal
$1/2$ teaspoon salt
1 teaspoon sugar
1 cup boiling water
1 cup milk
oil or butter for the griddle
butter
maple syrup

1. Combine the first three ingredients. Pour boiling water over the mixture very slowly to swell the meal. Let it sit for several minutes, then add enough milk (about 1 cup) so that the mixture will drop from a spoon.

2. Heat a lightly greased pancake griddle or cast-iron skillet and spoon batter onto the hot surface, leaving a few inches between each cake. Cook until golden, then turn to brown the other side, about 3 minutes more. Serve immediately with butter and real maple syrup.

PICKLED HERRING WITH MASHED POTATOES AND CARAMELIZED ONIONS

I trusted Joanne Neft's enthusiasm as well as her food sense but couldn't quite imagine cold herring on hot mashed potatoes until I made it. Well, it works. Add just a pinch of parsley and you have a lovely little supper. And if herring doesn't appeal to you, replace it with sautéed spinach or lentils or both.

2 or 3 teaspoons butter

1 large onion, white or yellow, sliced about ¼ inch thick

2 medium-size russet potatoes

salt and pepper

butter or sour cream

6-inch-long piece of pickled herring (not in sour cream), sliced into 4 or 5 attractive bite-size pieces

pinch of chopped parsley

1. Melt the butter in a 10-inch skillet. With the heat on medium-high, add the onions and give them a stir. Cook for about 10 minutes, stirring frequently, then add ¼ cup or so of water, cover the pan, and turn the heat to low. Every so often, give the onions a stir.

2. Meanwhile, peel and chunk the potatoes, then put them in a pan with cold water to cover and several big pinches of salt. Boil gently until they are tender when pierced with a knife, about 20 minutes. Scoop them out of the water and remove them to a bowl. Mash them with a few tablespoons of the cooking water, butter or sour cream to your taste, a splash of vinegar from the herring, and freshly ground pepper. Meanwhile, check the onions and season them with salt and pepper, too.

3. To serve, mound half the potatoes on a warm plate, making a little dome. Spoon half, or a little less, of the onions over the potatoes, then lay the herring pieces around the top. Add a spoonful of sour cream and a pinch of parsley. Enjoy with a salad, sautéed spinach, and a glass of chilled Riesling.

MAUREEN'S SHRIMP, FETA, AND BULGUR SALAD

Maureen Callahan is the rare nutritionist who forges good sense with good flavor. "I'm not a nut about 30 percent fat," she writes. "I'm more interested in just making fat the healthy variety. Add more if you like."

1. Combine the bulgur, water, and half the lemon juice in a small saucepan. Add a pinch of salt; bring to a boil. Cover and simmer for 18 to 20 minutes, or until tender. Drain and cool.

2. Sprinkle the shrimp with the rest of the lemon juice. Let stand 5 minutes, then stir in cucumber and the next 5 ingredients. Add the lemon zest and toss gently. Stir in the cooled bulgur. Season with salt and pepper, sprinkle with feta, and serve.

- ¼ cup medium-size bulgur
- ¾ cup water
- 1 lemon, zest and 1½ tablespoons juice
- salt and pepper
- 5 cooked and peeled large shrimp, coarsely chopped
- ¼ cup peeled diced cucumber
- ½ cup cherry tomatoes, halved
- 1 green onion, including a little of the green, finely sliced
- 2 tablespoons chopped parsley
- ½ tablespoon finely chopped mint or oregano
- 1 tablespoon extra-virgin olive oil
- 1 tablespoon crumbled feta cheese

OMELET WITH CRUNCHY
BUTTERED BREADCRUMBS

Serving your eggs with crunchy buttered breadcrumbs instead of having them with a piece of buttered toast is a little change that makes a big difference. It can make the most mundane eggs somehow special, whether fried or made into an omelet. Enjoy with a big clump of watercress sprinkled with sea salt and fresh lemon juice if you like.

**1 slice of your favorite
 kind of bread
butter
2 or 3 fresh eggs, gently
 beaten with a fork
salt and pepper**

The Breadcrumbs: Cut the crusts off the bread and discard. Pulse the bread in a food processor to make coarse crumbs. Melt 2 or 3 teaspoons butter in a small skillet over medium heat, add the crumbs, and stir them around. Cook, stirring occasionally, for probably at least 5 minutes, until they're crisp and crunchy, then slide them onto a plate.

The Omelet: Season the eggs with a few pinches of salt and some freshly ground pepper. Return the pan to the heat, raise the temperature, add a bit more butter, and wait until the foam subsides. Pour in the eggs, let them sit for a few seconds, then begin pulling the outside into the center, tilting the pan so that the uncooked egg falls back onto the hot surface. When the eggs are cooked to your liking, give the omelet a flip, sprinkle some of the breadcrumbs over the top, then slide the omelet onto your plate, folding it in two as you do so. Add the rest of the crumbs to the top, more pepper if you desire, and sit down to dinner.

The same crunchy bread–crumbs that enhanced the previous recipe do the same for this frittata. Add a vegetable on the side, such as tomatoes, simmered asparagus, or sautéed mushrooms.

3 eggs

salt and pepper

1/2 cup ricotta cheese

freshly grated Parmigiano-Reggiano

1 tablespoon chopped fresh herbs, such as
 parsley, marjoram, or oregano

1 small garlic clove, crushed

butter

crispy breadcrumbs

1. Beat the eggs with a few pinches of salt and freshly ground pepper. Stir in the cheeses, herb, and garlic.

2. Melt 2 or more teaspoons butter in an 8-inch skillet over medium-high heat. When it bubbles and foams, add the egg mixture and lower the heat. Give the pan a shake to make sure the mixture's not sticking, then cook until set, about 4 or 5 minutes. Slide the half-cooked eggs onto a plate, keeping the cooked side facing down. Set the pan over them, then grasping both pan and plate with a hot pad, flip them over and cook the second side.

3. When done, slide the frittata onto a plate, sprinkle with the bread–crumbs, and serve.

This is so quick, warm, and nourishing that it can easily become habit-forming. I'm already making it on a regular basis. Tomatoes on toast are more substantial than, say, a tomato soup with croutons, and lighter than full-blown tomato rarebit with cheese. The toast starts out crisp but turns nice and mushy as you eat—a little like a cheater's version of *papa al pomodoro*. Canned diced organic tomatoes work perfectly fine for the months of the year (which is most of them) when good fresh ones aren't to be had. A 15-ounce can provides for a generous serving for one, leaving extra spoonfuls to stir into scrambled eggs or noodles.

1 (15-ounce) can diced organic tomatoes

butter or olive oil

1 garlic clove, pressed

your favorite bread, toasted

salt and pepper

sugar, if needed

1 teaspoon Worcestershire sauce or
   2 to 3 teaspoons cream or crème fraîche

fresh chopped herbs, if available, such as
   parsley or basil

a chunk of Parmesan cheese for grating

1. Heat a small skillet over medium-high heat and add the entire contents of the can of tomatoes. Add a dab of butter or a splash of olive oil, and press in the garlic clove. Give it a stir and simmer while you toast your bread.

2. Taste and season the tomatoes with salt and freshly ground pepper. If they're very tart, add a pinch or two of sugar. Stir in the Worcestershire sauce or 2 to 3 teaspoons cream plus any herbs.

3. Cut the toast into 2 or 3 pieces and lay it in a shallow soup plate. Spoon your tomatoes over the toast. Add a little more pepper and grate some cheese over the top.

SOME VARIATIONS

Tomatoes on toast invite you to play. Add such things as a smidgen of curry powder, other fresh herbs (tarragon, lovage, dill, or snipped chives), or a spoonful of leftover herb butter (page 122). If the tomatoes need a flavor boost, stir in a teaspoon of tomato paste, and if you like cheese with your tomatoes— Gorgonzola, fresh mozzarella, Cheddar—cube some and drop the pieces into the pan. The cheese will soften and ease itself into the tomatoes. If you're using fresh tomatoes, drop them into boiling water for about 10 seconds, then peel off the skins. Halve them crosswise, pull out the seeds with your fingers, then cut them into dice.

SAUTÉED MUSHROOMS FOR TOAST, POLENTA, OR PASTA

There are a lot of ways to approach something as simple as sautéed mushrooms. For example, you can use olive oil, butter, or both for fat; you can include a few dried wild mushrooms for flavor, or not; you can just buy a bag of sliced white mushrooms or cook with an assortment of mushrooms; you can douse them with a splash of sherry or wine; and finally, you can finish with a touch of cream or sour cream or nothing at all. This version peps up regular white mushrooms with a few dried porcini. But regardless of which little changes you make, these mushrooms are easily prepared and, once you have them, as handy as can be. They can go over toast, polenta, rice, potatoes, or pasta, or in an omelet. An 8-ounce package of mushrooms yields about 1 cup cooked.

1 tablespoon dried porcini, more or less

½ cup boiling water

½ onion

1 garlic clove

a dozen parsley sprigs

1 tablespoon butter, olive oil, or a mixture

pinch dried thyme

1 (8- to 10-ounce) bag sliced mushrooms
   or whole mushrooms, sliced

salt and pepper

splash of sherry or wine

squirt of tomato paste, about a teaspoon

spoonful of cream or
   crème fraîche (optional)

1. Cover the dried mushrooms with the boiling water and set them aside while you dice the onion and chop the garlic and parsley together.

2. Melt the butter in a 10-inch skillet over medium heat. Add the onion, thyme, and half the parsley mixture, and give it a stir. Lift the rehydrated mushrooms out of their liquid and add them to the onion along with a few tablespoons of the soaking liquid. Cook for 5 minutes, then add the fresh mushrooms and raise the heat. Sprinkle mushrooms with ¼ teaspoon salt, then turn them in the pan. Cook, turning every 30 seconds or so, until browned here and there, about 4 minutes. Add a few splashes sherry or wine, stir in the tomato paste, and cook for about 30 seconds. Add the rest of the mushroom liquid (poured through a fine sieve) and the parsley.

3. Lower the heat and cook less vigorously for about 5 minutes. Taste. Add more salt if needed and season with pepper. Just before you're ready to serve, stir in a little cream or crème fraîche, if using.

MUSHROOMS ON TOAST

Toast a piece of levain bread or ciabatta, then cover it with thin slices of aged cheese, such as Gouda, Gruyère, or Manchego. Set the toast on your plate and spoon the sautéed mushrooms (page 164) and their juices over the toast. Sprinkle on the remaining parsley mixture and more pepper.

MUSHROOMS WITH TOMATOES OVER POLENTA

Follow the recipe for sautéed mushrooms (page 164). Once you've cooked off the wine, add ½ cup (about ½ small can) diced organic tomatoes. Include the juice too—it's nice to have some broth to moisten the polenta or whatever starchy item you choose to use here. In winter, you might add ½ teaspoon minced rosemary when you start the onions, or a few pinches dried thyme. In summer, finish the dish with a chiffonade of basil leaves. At any time, end with a fresh grating of good Parmesan cheese.

MUSHROOMS IN PAPRIKA CREAM OVER EGG NOODLES

Follow the recipe for sautéed mushrooms (page 164). Stir in ¼ cup crème fraîche or sour cream just at the end, long enough to warm it, along with ½ teaspoon sweet Hungarian or smoked Spanish paprika. Serve the mushrooms over flat egg noodles.

ROASTED SWEET POTATOES WITH GOAT CHEESE

This sounds simple and it is simple because many of us like to make a meal of just one vegetable. However, the combination of tangy goat cheese with the sweet, moist orange-fleshed potatoes (it must be these and not the drier white-fleshed varieties) works well, the sweet and salty flavors colliding under a crunchy sprinkle of sea salt. Good enough to share, and often. Add a salad and you've got a meal.

sweet potatoes, such as jewel or garnet yams (yes, they really are sweet potatoes)

fresh, tangy goat cheese

salt and pepper

1. Heat oven to 375 degrees F. Select your potatoes (smaller ones will cook more quickly) and scrub them well. Poke them in a few places with a paring knife, then put them in a shallow baking dish and bake until tender, about 1½ hours for large tubers, 1 hour for medium-size skinny ones, and 30 minutes for those tiny 3-inch sweet potatoes one can occasionally find. Or steam them over boiling water, which takes less time.

2. While the potatoes are roasting, allow the cheese to come to room temperature. When they're done, slice them in half, season with salt and freshly ground pepper, then soften up the flesh with a fork. Lay some goat cheese over those hot middles, add a little more pepper, and enjoy.

CHAPTER 8

Alone Every Day

"I eat alone all the time in this my seventy-ninth year, and I love to eat alone! Nobody to please but myself."
—Betty Fussell, *writer*

"Eating alone is a hard thing. It's hard to energize yourself to do it when it's just you."
—Nick Ault, *private eye*

THERE ARE PEOPLE WHO GO THROUGH LIFE without a daily dining companion, those who never marry or form a partnership. Young people, just out in the world, working their first jobs or toiling on graduate degrees, frequently don't have partners other than roommates. Then there are slightly older singles who, maybe in their thirties or early forties, just haven't gotten around to finding someone to settle down with. The years after divorce but before a new marriage are a time when one returns to eating alone, and there are those years at the end of one's life when a partner is lost and one is alone again. In these cases, solo meals are not the fruit of those rare and welcomed spells when a spouse is out of town or the kids are away. This is when every night is likely to be an eat-alone night—

unless something is done about it. A friend of ours, for example, made sure that after her husband died she had a reservation for herself and one of her many friends at a restaurant practically every night of the week. While people deal with these periods in their lives in very different ways, for many it is a challenge that is hard to meet. Others meet it with grace and style.

Laura Calder is a young woman who lives in Paris part of the year. She writes about food in France today, and she has a television show on French cooking in her native Canada. Cooking is a big part of her life.

"But the fact of the matter is, I don't cook much for myself," Laura writes, admitting that she is usually the queen of grilled cheese sandwiches when left in her own company. "Instead, I throw dinner parties and cook for other people. But lately I have been living in a place where you couldn't pay me to throw a dinner party, so I have found myself cooking for me. The other day I made a huge Swiss chard gratin and ate the whole thing (half for lunch, the other half for dinner). And tonight, like at least three other nights a week, I made a pan of **roasted vegetables**, grated over some Parmesan cheese, and gobbled them up. I change vegetable combinations all the time, just to keep life edgy: sometimes it's root vegetables (potatoes, beets), more often there are leeks involved, and lately I am obsessed with fennel and aubergine. The secret to great roasted vegetables, no matter what the combination, is to chuck in a few handfuls of cherry tomatoes. They're the ticket, because they really caramelize and get sticky and sweet and go great with whatever else you've got on the sheet."

Laura also has her favorite eat-alone sauce, **blue cheese sauce.** "While the pasta boils or the steak fries or whatever, you get a little saucepan, plop in a few spoonfuls of crème fraîche, then add tons of blue cheese and let it all melt together. Instant and delicious. Ugly as all hell, however. But who's looking?"

What an appealing strategy, and how easy—quantities of vegetables, pasta, or a steak, simply cooked and then uplifted with rich blue-cheesy sauce. The sauce is also fabulous on polenta, especially if you use Gorgonzola cheese, but even if you don't, it's awfully good. Try it on steamed broccoli—you won't believe that broccoli can be so delicious.

Peggy Knickerbocker, our writer-cook friend in San Francisco, mentions some snacky solutions for some of her daily solo meals. "That is," she qualifies, "if I'm not making a green salad with seared tuna." But when she's eating a more snack-like meal, she might have popcorn with olive oil and sea salt, or, if she's on a sweet track, she'll go for frozen yogurt with angel food cake and a peach. But Peggy also tells us how she might make a **farmers market salad**, if she's not into snacking or searing tuna. "In this case," she says, waving her hand toward a half-dozen French bowls and fruit plates heaped with spring vegetables from the morning's trip to San Francisco's Ferry Plaza Market, "I'd make a salad of fresh shucked peas, shaved artichokes, fennel, and shavings of Parmigiano-Reggiano. It's so good. What else do you need?" she asks us, and we can't think of a thing, except maybe a glass of wine and a hunk of bread. Or maybe her salad *is* enough.

Laura and Peggy both cook for others frequently, and cook well for themselves, albeit simply, when eating alone. But more commonly, single people struggle with feeding themselves. A private eye named Nick Ault, who now works as a cop, is hardly alone in his predicament, which is having to wrestle a nasty schedule. He works three twelve-hour days in a row, followed by three days off, which creates a somewhat imbalanced schedule for cooking and eating. The days he's working, cooking is impossible.

"Those days it's hot dogs. A couple of dogs a day," Nick drawls, then shrugs and adds, "What can I do?"

But despite the dog-dog routine, Nick is pretty sophisticated about food. He's been exposed to a lot of good cooking, and he likes eating out, preferably at a restaurant's bar, where he can rustle up some conversation as well as dinner. Nick can also rustle up a steak for himself and serve it with a sliced tomato salad. But more impressive than

a steak, and quite in contrast to his double-dog days, is his Bolognese sauce.

"The key to making a good Bolognese," he explains, "is taking your time with the *mise en place*, and enjoying the whole process. I take time to hand cut the vegetables, I get all the different kinds of ground meats the recipe requires, and I play a little opera—it adds to my enthusiasm. I use Pomi tomatoes and finish with a little cream. Then I eat off of it for several meals. I eat it on pasta or on polenta. It's really good."

When we ask Nick when he had last made his Bolognese sauce, he pauses, counts, then reveals it's probably been at least six months. Again, he shrugs. "Eating alone is a hard thing. Peanut butter and jelly sandwiches with a bag of potato chips—that would be a meal. It's hard to energize yourself to do it when it's just you. So I guess I just get lazy."

It is hard for many of us to look forward to cooking a meal that's just for ourselves. It's not just laziness, but some feeling that it's not quite worth the effort when it's just for us. That *we're* not worth it! I hear this over and over. The hardest thing ever for me was writing cookbooks when I was unhappily single. It was so joyless to be cooking all this food, trying to really taste it, and then eat it or give it away. When people say they take the time to shop and cook well for themselves, that they don't stint when it comes to solo meals, or deny themselves good food and wine, there's something self-respectful and positive in that. But it's oddly rare. We seem to have little tolerance for such pleasures.

"I shop a lot," muses Nick's former wife, our friend and neighbor, "but I really don't cook a lot." Chase also knows a lot about cooking, having been professionally involved with food for many years. She always has a cold bottle of Tattinger in her fridge and is quick to offer a glass.

"Basically I end up making soups and stew with whatever I have," she says, "and I always have potatoes, onions, garlic, celery, and carrots on hand, so I can do that. Sometimes I plan ahead for certain vegetables, like parsnips or butternut squash, but no matter what, everything goes into one dish."

A universal stew. In fact, we call it Chase's Universal.

Along with the vegetables, Chase usually has ground beef on hand, and that goes in her stew, too. "If I add green pepper, that turns it into chili. Add oregano and it's suddenly a filling for tacos." She continues enumerating the little additions that push her dish in one direction or another. One time we had her stew in the form of pasta sauce, sort of a rough Bolognese, in fact. It was hearty and good. She served it with a crunchy **salad of celery and olives**, which she learned from an Italian friend. "But," she confesses, "I don't make that for myself alone." Instead she sticks with her one-pot meal and is happy with that.

One woman not in possession of such a simple approach to her dine-alone menu as Chase's Universal, described a three-tiered way of eating that reflects the obvious, that we're just not the same from day to day. "I always eat alone because I live alone," Lynn says, "but every night is different, depending on the day's events. The best, most desirable dinners start with an early arrival home and groceries in the fridge already. Or, time to shop. I grill a chop, make a salad, cook a favorite vegetable, or bake a potato. I'm in front of the TV in time for *The Closer*. In summer I watch the world outside my window. Sometimes when I'm hungry for both food and the act of cooking, I'll make something like short ribs, knowing that I'll eat very late. Those leftovers make a meal I can look forward to during the week."

For the second tier: "When I'm tired and sad, I make a fried egg sandwich with Pepperidge Farm's very thin white bread and watch reruns of *Law and Order*."

And the third tier: "I eat a pint of chocolate ice cream and watch whatever's on."

I once stood in Whole Foods on a Saturday night and watched an obviously single woman order the inevitable skinless, boneless chicken breast from the butcher. It felt so sad that I immediately wanted to invite her home to eat with us instead, but of course I had no idea who she was and vice versa. Had I known her, I would have at least told her about Laura's blue cheese sauce, but that would undo the so-called virtuous bit about the breast being skinless. Curiously, despite the hundreds of times boneless, skinless chicken breasts are glowingly described in women's magazines as the answer to the single girl's meal and weight-loss plan, not one woman we spoke with brought up this dispirited food as a culinary possibility.

Another better version, and one you can eat off of for a few meals, is the roasted bone-in chicken breast, with the skin attached. You can roast it as you would a whole bird, though in less time, then you can have half of it for dinner and carve the second half into slices for sandwiches or a salad. Being on the bone and with the skin, it has much more flavor.

ONE
BONELESS
SKINLESS
CHICKEN
BREAST

And a whole roast chicken, another favorite for the constant solo diner, takes one even further. If you cook your own, you have the advantage of filling your house with good smells while it's in the oven. Peggy Markel, a good cook who mostly lives in Italy except for twice-yearly visits to her home in Colorado, says that when she's home she likes to roast a chicken, "because then I can eat it in different ways. I like it hot and moist, just when it comes out of the oven. I always eat a few bits while standing up. Then I put it on a plate with whatever else I have—roasted potatoes or salad. I eat the leftovers on a rye cracker with butter and a little lettuce on top." And then she makes a stock with whatever else is left and uses it to make a risotto.

The practical theme of having one big thing to eat from runs through many solutions to meal after meal alone. A pot of soup. Chase's Universal. A ton of Bolognese sauce. Then there's the "pot of something starchy" approach to solo eating, and usually it's rice. Indeed, the very blandness of rice makes it a gift. Of course it's better cooked fresh each time, but even leftovers can prove useful. My mother vigorously touts the virtues of having a pot of rice on hand at all times. "Cook two or more cups of brown (or white) rice," she suggests, "keep it covered in a bowl in the refrigerator and use it for the next two or three days. It's a wonderful backup, whether you want it with milk for breakfast, rice pudding for dessert, or as something to go with a Chinese recipe."

One of her favorite things to do with her waiting bowl of rice is to fry it up with tofu and green pepper, spinach, and perhaps a beaten egg to bind it all together. "And a dash of soy sauce," she adds. (Curiously, this is what I used to eat in college day after day, but it's nothing we ever ate as a family.)

The idea of using rice to make a little **rice pudding** is a good one. Heat it with milk; add raisins, brown sugar, or maple syrup, and cinnamon; and you have a sweet, comforting dish that's reasonably good for you. Add a bit of butter, a glug of cream, or a dollop of crème fraîche and it's even better. A more exotic rice pudding can be made from basmati rice laced with honey, pistachios, and saffron. That's dinner and dessert in one. And leftover rice can also be turned into a soothing sort of congee, a savory rice porridge with bits of vegetables, tofu, or meat.

Among some of the youngish single people who really do like to cook for themselves is Maureen Callahan of the bulgur and shrimp salad. "I have a lot of single friends who hate to cook for just themselves," she says, "but not me. I love to cook and it doesn't matter if I'm the only audience. I find it relaxing to chop fresh vegetables and hang out in my kitchen, concocting a special meal for myself. I turn on some good music and I'm in heaven."

One of the things that does matter to Maureen are the ingredients she cooks with. "My sister just about passed out at the total for my grocery bill when she went shopping with me, but I splurge on good ingredients. Cooking is fun when you're trying a new olive oil or vinegar, a new variety of heirloom vegetables. It's a voyage of discovery."

Some young people have told us that they prefer to eat out with their friends rather than cook, and Maureen did too when she lived in Boston. Looking back on her days in graduate school, she recalls, "An older friend of mine cooked at home all the time and was always turning down dinner invitations. Back then, I wanted to try all the hip new places and explore all the ethnic restaurants, so I didn't understand. Sarah was kind of a curmudgeon about dining out. If the restaurant wasn't exceptional, she didn't want to waste her money. And now I'm starting to feel the same way. I can cook a piece of fish a whole lot better than a lot of restaurants. Plus, I know exactly what's going into my meal in regards to nutrition and the environment. I like knowing where my food comes from and whom I'm supporting. I guess as I get older there's a lot more wrapped up in my cooking decisions."

A Santa Fe cook echoed Maureen's thoughts when she said that she finds restaurants are more and more disappointing. "I would rather prepare food myself, even if it does mean eating alone," says Marilyn Ferrell, who owned a Mexican restaurant for twenty years before retiring to Santa Fe. "I have been known to have my freshly made guacamole with organic blue-sesame corn chips and a drink, and that's dinner a couple of times a week," she confesses. "And since an avocado is never the same after it's opened and I must eat the whole thing, it leaves no room for anything else. But just think of all that potassium I am getting!"

But a few times a week Marilyn makes a more complete meal for herself. "A piece of broiled fish with a topping, a baked potato, and my favorite vegetables with garlic and olive oil. I make enough vegetables to last for a couple of meals. Or I make a pot of navy beans and ham, and eat standing up in the kitchen, savoring each bite."

And if Marilyn wants a particular food that she doesn't eat often, she says, "Being alone would not stop me from preparing it, even if I give away some to another solo friend. Especially when it comes to a dessert I want to make. I make it, eat some, and give it away." And it's not a bad thing to be on the receiving end of one of Marilyn's desserts.

For older people especially, being alone often suddenly involves a new way of living, a life that's rudely jarring in its unfamiliarity. We have heard from so many older people who make do with a carton of yogurt, something tossed in a microwave, or a bowl of cereal, that it's disheartening. The light just seems to go out when food is no longer about shared meals and conversation. For many of us, eating is a very social act, one that thrives on company, even that of one other person.

"Very sad things happen to older people when they lose their partners," writes Marsha Weiner, thinking of her own grandparents. "Some just can't get a grip on feeding themselves well when suddenly alone. It's just too foreign."

But that's not always the case. After Rosalind Cummins talked about her own cobbled together meals that she sometimes shares with her cat, Tiny, she sighed and added, "My dad used to make a real dinner for himself every night after my mom died, and I really admired him for that. He was a fabulous cook. There were many dishes he made from memory, but he also cooked out of the *New York Times* pretty often. I really miss his cooking. Nobody makes Finnan Haddie for me anymore!"

I was moved by Judith Jones's thoughts in her book, *The Tenth Muse,* on cooking and eating alone after Evan, her husband of so many years and partner in so many adventurous meals, died. At first she doubted that she could cook again, but then found that enacting what had been for the two of them a daily ritual was actually a way of bringing Evan back into what had been their shared life—walking into the kitchen at the end of the day, turning on music, and conjuring up an enjoyable evening meal.

"When, at last, I sit down and light the candles," she writes, "the place across from me is not empty." These words strike me as an eloquent defense of the value that comes of cooking and enjoying the pleasures of the table.

"I actually enjoy preparing my simple meals," my ninety-year-old mother says. "They must be working out well because I feel great most of the time. And I'm so glad that the nutritionists have decided that coffee is very good for you and that you should drink a lot of it, because coffee is my preferred drink."

My mother has been eating alone for a great many years except when she invites friends over to dinner, which is often. A soup enthusiast, she reminds me about a saying of her mother's, which was "two and two make five," meaning a soup can be taken a long way from what you start with. You can change it over the three or four days it's around, having it chunky one night, puréed the next, adding cream a third night, croutons and garnishes a fourth. And that's exactly what a lot of solo eaters do because when you want to eat but don't want to think about cooking, soup is that dish. It's extremely accommodating, mostly agreeing to improve with age. But then, the soup my mother turns to over and over again is not one of these mathematical soups, but a **salmon chowder**, which hearkens back to her Rhode Island roots.

For a year I took care of an elderly woman who was recovering from an illness. Her spotless, all-white apartment offered an expansive view of San Francisco Bay and the ships slowly going in and out all day long. She took her simple meals at her highly polished table, eating with silver designed by her architect husband. Every day I made her well-balanced little dishes, but what she craved every afternoon was a warm froth of egg yolks, sugar, and Marsala—*Zabaglione*. She claimed that it gave her strength. I can't imagine a more delicious and delicate way to gain strength, and when I'm her age, I plan to do exactly the same thing.

Certainly cooking for oneself day in and day out is very different than the occasional night at home alone if for no other reason than it endures. And not every person likes her own company at the table on an ongoing basis. Still, sustained solo eating does have its enthusiasts.

"I eat alone about two hundred nights a year," says Sylvia Thompson, who then goes on to list a far-reaching range of foods that she cooks, from elaborate pastas to all kinds of salads and vegetables, occasional soups, and frequent frittatas. "But," she writes, "there are the nights when I just have bread and cheese, eaten out of hand standing in the kitchen." Certainly there has to be a certain amount of pleasure present to be able and willing to deploy so many means of feeding oneself.

"I eat alone all the time in this my seventy-ninth year, and I *love* to eat alone!" says another writer, Betty Fussell. "Nobody to please but myself."

Here's how her solo cooking and dining goes.

"I open the door of the fridge and look inside. It's always exciting, so many little things forgotten at the back of shelves. What can I put together for this improvised, unrepeatable, once-in-a-lifetime meal? Ah, there's half a lemon, here's a wrinkled poblano chile, there's

a barely used container of heavy cream. With
any luck there'll be a few sprigs of
coriander in a plastic sandwich bag.
Could use some tomatillos, but
don't see any. Drat. However, I
know there're some pumpkin
seeds in a bag in the freezer.
There's always garlic and onion
in a basket on the coun-
ter. Doesn't take long
to char the poblano,

toast the seeds, sauté the garlic, and throw everything in the
blender with some chicken bouillon if the stuff is too thick. Taste and
taste again for seasoning. A little Mexican oregano? Okay. I've got a
dried pack in the fridge. Balance salt with lemon and black pepper.
Yeah, that's coming along. Check the TV page. What's on TCM? Time
the heating of my cream of poblano soup with Showtime. Take soup
on tray with a nice cold Sancerre. Prop up the pillows on the bed.
Click on the remote. Any night can be the Saturday movie matinee of
my childhood—except that I get to have Real Food at the same time
instead of making a melting Mars bar last for an hour and a half."

It's got to be rare, or tuna will be dry and unappealing. The sparkly green salsa verde brightens the tuna. Set your steak on a bed of interesting greens that drift toward the peppery end of the spectrum—small red mustard leaves, watercress, land cress, arugula—and repeat the oil and lemon theme in the dressing. They do what a dab of wasabi does, which is to wake up your nose and make the delicate tuna better by contrast.

**salsa verde with lemon and
  capers (page 185)**
1 tuna steak
olive oil
salt and pepper
2 handfuls spicy salad greens
1 lemon

1. Make the salsa verde first. Coat the tuna on both sides with olive oil, then season well with salt and freshly ground pepper. Wash and dry your greens and have them ready to dress with olive oil and lemon.

2. Heat a cast-iron skillet over medium-high heat until it feels hot when you hold your hand over it. Add olive oil to coat, then the steak. Cook for 1½ minutes, then turn and cook 1½ minutes on the other side. This should be enough, but look at the tuna itself from the side. When done, you should see a thin white line where the fish met the pan and a large pink area in the middle bordered by another white line.

3. During that last minute, dress your salad, tossing it with a pinch of salt, olive oil to coat lightly, and a squeeze of lemon. Put the salad on your plate, lay the tuna steak on top, and spoon the salsa verde over it.

You can use any leftovers from three-minute tuna to make a tuna salad. Flake a chunk of the tuna with your fingers, season it with a little salt, then dress it with more salsa verde, mayonnaise, or a lemon vinaigrette. Add something crisp—such as finely diced celery. Pile it on a mound of lettuce or, for a change, a bed of shaved fennel. You can also use leftover tuna to make the tuna spread (page 97).

SALSA VERDE WITH LEMON AND CAPERS

Use a wedge of lemon instead of just the zest and juice to make a bright lemony sauce to use over seared tuna, under scallops, and in a million other places you can think of, from sandwiches to soups. A sweet Meyer lemon is ideal. If using the more acidic Eureka lemon, you might want to correct its tartness by adding a little more oil at the end.

¼ cup finely chopped parsley
   or chervil
2 scallions, including a little of the
   green, finely chopped, or one
   shallot, finely diced
⅛ lemon, preferably a Meyer lemon,
   finely sliced
2 teaspoons capers, rinsed
2 to 3 tablespoons extra-virgin olive oil
salt

Combine all the ingredients except the salt in a bowl. Stir them together, add salt to taste and more olive oil to loosen the herbs, if needed.

More elaborate than other salads you might make from a farmers market, such as sliced tomatoes with basil, this recipe takes artichokes, new potatoes, a bulb of fennel, and a fresh farm egg and turns them into a meal. Because there's only one of you to cook for, it really doesn't take all that long, plus you can overlap the different steps. To me, these vegetables cry for tarragon, chervil, or another licorice-flavored herb.

THE VEGETABLES

4 fingerling potatoes, scrubbed

salt and pepper

4 baby artichokes

1 lemon

1 fresh egg

1 small fennel bulb

THE LEMON-HERB DRESSING

grated zest and 2 to 3 teaspoons juice of 1 lemon

1 shallot, finely diced

a few pinches salt

3 tablespoons olive oil

1 teaspoon finely chopped parsley

1 teaspoon finely chopped tarragon

1. Put the potatoes in a pot, cover them with cold water, add ½ teaspoon salt, and bring to a boil. Lower the heat and cook until tender when pierced with a knife, about 20 minutes, depending on their size. When they're done, remove them, but keep the water in the pot.

2. While the potatoes are cooking, snap off the outer leaves of the artichokes until you get to the pale green soft-looking ones. Trim the base and the stem, cut off the top third of the leaves, then slice the artichokes lengthwise in thirds. As you work, put them in a bowl of water with the lemon juice. When all are ready, place them in the potato

water and boil gently until tender when pierced with a knife, 12 to 15 minutes. They should be evenly colored when done, not blotchy. Drain and set aside.

3. Put the egg in a small pot, cover with cold water, bring to a boil, and boil for 1 minute. Cover the pot and let stand for 6 minutes more, then drain. Rinse, then peel, the egg.

4. Make the lemon-herb dressing by combining the lemon zest and juice, shallot, and salt in a small bowl. Whisk in the oil, then add the herbs. Taste and adjust, adding more oil or lemon as needed to get the right balance.

5. To compose the salad, grate the fennel on a box grater into paper-thin slices and scatter them on a plate. Drizzle a little of the dressing over the fennel and season it with a few pinches of salt. Separately dress the artichokes and potatoes, then scatter them over the fennel. Quarter the egg and tuck the pieces in among the vegetables. Have with a good piece of bread and, perhaps, some cheese from your farmers market.

ROAST BONE-IN, SKIN-ON CHICKEN BREASTS
WITH HERB BUTTER

Both the bone and skin add flavor, and the skin provides a nifty little pocket in which you can tuck herbs, spices, and flavorings of all sorts. If you can only find a split breast, then use that. Roast some diced summer or winter vegetables at the same time; have them with the chicken.

1 whole bone-in chicken breast, about 1½ pounds

1½ tablespoons butter, at room temperature

salt and pepper

grated zest of 1 lemon

2 teaspoons finely chopped rosemary or sage

1 garlic clove, minced

1. Preheat the oven to 450 degrees F. Pat the chicken dry, then gently loosen the skin with your hands.

2. Mix the butter with ¼ teaspoon salt, pepper, lemon zest, rosemary or sage, and garlic. Spread it under the skin and over the meat.

3. Season the whole breast well with salt and freshly ground pepper, then set the breast, skin side up, on a foil-lined sheet pan or in a baking dish. Roast for 35 minutes, or until the meat thermometer registers 160 degrees at the thickest part of the breast. Take it out of the oven, let stand for 5 minutes, then carve off as much as you wish to eat. Wrap and refrigerate the rest for your next dish.

Given that this guacamole, along with some blue corn chips or a warm tortilla, might be your dinner, it has more tomato than normal, making it a bit more salady.

Chop the onion, cilantro, and chile with 1/4 teaspoon salt to make a rough paste. Pit, peel, and mash the avocado with a fork, keeping it chunky. Add the onion mixture and tomatoes, season with half the lime juice, then taste and add more, if needed.

1 heaping tablespoon finely diced white onion

2 tablespoons chopped cilantro

1 scant teaspoon finely diced jalapeño chile

salt

1 avocado

1 tomato, seeded and diced

1 teaspoon lime juice, to taste

Summer vegetables, including freshly dug potatoes and carrots, have more moisture than winter's roots, so chances are they'll cook much faster. Just be sure to give them lots of room so that they don't crowd each other. Here are some amounts to get you started, but they're hardly absolute and certainly varieties can be mixed—yellow, green, and black zucchini or pattypans; cipollini, torpedo, or regular old yellow onions, and so forth. There's enough here for more than one meal. Leftovers make a great room-temperature salad.

1 medium-size eggplant, cut into
    wedges or cubes
salt and pepper
4 fingerling potatoes, scrubbed
2 zucchini, halved lengthwise and cut into
    2-inch sections
2 large carrots, peeled and sliced into
    ¼-inch rounds
1 head garlic, cloves separated but
    not peeled
1 or 2 bell peppers, cut into long
    inch-wide strips
1 large or 3 small onions, peeled, cut into
    wedges with the root ends attached
2 handfuls cherry tomatoes, stems removed
olive oil
chopped herbs, such as thyme, rosemary,
    oregano, parsley

1. Toss the eggplant with ½ teaspoon of salt and set aside in a colander to drain. Preheat oven to 400 degrees F. While it's heating, wash and cut the rest of the vegetables and put them in a bowl.

2. Once the oven is hot, quickly rinse the eggplant and blot it dry, then add it to the bowl. Toss with enough oil to moisten, about 3 or 4 tablespoons, and season with salt and freshly ground pepper.

3. Spread the vegetables out onto a sheet pan, then put in the center of the oven and roast until they've colored in places and become tender, about 25 minutes, turning them once or twice while cooking. Remove and scatter fresh herbs over all. Serve hot or tepid.

Sometimes roasting just one or two vegetables is perfect. But it's also fun to have a mix, and you've got a lot of very tasty, rooty options during the fall and winter months. Like what? Rutabagas and turnips, winter squash, celery root, parsnips, and, not to be overlooked, Jerusalem artichokes. If they're available, take Laura Calder's suggestion and throw in a handful of cherry tomatoes.

Although the preparation is easy enough, it does take 45 minutes to roast dense roots that have been cut into large chunks. And because they do take a while, I suggest preparing enough to turn some into a roasted vegetable chowder—at least eight cups of prepared vegetables, as they will shrink to almost half their volume.

2 or 3 carrots, peeled and cut into large chunks, then halved lengthwise (or left whole, if small)

1 russet potato or several fingerlings, scrubbed and chunked

1 onion, cut into thick wedges (keep the root end intact)

1 head garlic, peeled and cloves separated

1 turnip, peeled only if gnarly, and cut into wedges

6 Jerusalem artichokes, scrubbed and halved

1 large parsnip, peeled, cut into 2-inch rounds and halved, core removed

a handful of cherry tomatoes, if available

2 tablespoons olive oil

salt and pepper

Two tips: To get lots of good caramelization, give your vegetables plenty of room so that they don't sit on top of one another. And if you think you'll make soup with the leftovers, include an extra carrot to use as a garnish.

Preheat the oven to 425 degrees F. Choose a large baking dish or sheet pan so that the vegetables can bake in a single layer. Cut the vegetables, then toss them with the oil, and season with a scant teaspoon salt and freshly ground pepper. Tip them into the baking dish. Roast until the vegetables are caramelized in places and tender when pierced with a knife. Give them a shake or a turn every 15 minutes or so, roasting about 45 minutes in all. These are delicious just as they are when they come out of the oven. In fact, it's hard to stop eating them. But they're also delicious served with a garlic mayonnaise.

ROASTED VEGETABLE CHOWDER

With 2 to 3 cups of leftover vegetables, you can make a quart of roasted vegetable chowder. Here's how. Put the vegetables, except for 6 or so reserved carrot pieces, in a saucepan, add 3½ cups water or stock and ½ teaspoon salt. Bring to a boil, then simmer for 15 minutes. Purée. The chowder will be very beige and thick, not very pretty looking, but don't worry. Return the purée to the soup pan and thin with extra water or stock. To make the soup sing, stir in a quarter cup of cream or half-and-half, leaving it streaky. Taste for salt and add more if needed. Dice the reserved carrots and mince a little parsley. Ladle the soup into bowls, add the carrots, sprinkle with parsley, and finish with freshly ground pepper.

This makes enough for just one large or two modest portions since fish soup isn't something people generally want to eat three or four days running. Smoked paprika gives it not only a wood–fire flavor but also a rosy background hue. With the pink fish, yellow potatoes, and green parsley flecks, this is a pretty, spring-like chowder.

1 tablespoon butter

½ cup diced onion

1 celery stalk, peeled and chopped

1 sprig thyme or a pinch dried thyme

1 bay leaf

8 ounces Yukon gold or russet potatoes, peeled and cut into 1-inch chunks

2 teaspoons each chopped parsley and celery leaves

½ teaspoon smoked or regular paprika

salt and pepper

2 cups milk, fish stock, or water

half-and-half to finish

1 chunk salmon, cut into large bite-size pieces, 4 to 6 ounces

1. Melt the butter in a small soup pot or saucepan and add the onion, celery, thyme, and bay leaf. Give it a stir, leave for a minute or two, and then add the potatoes and half the parsley mixture. Season with the paprika and ½ teaspoon of salt. Cook over medium heat for 5 minutes or so, occasionally stirring.

2. Add the milk, stock, or water. Bring to a boil, then cover the pot and simmer until the potatoes are tender. Mash a few of them against the sides of the pan to give the soup body. At this point, enrich the soup with a little half-and-half or more milk, if desired. Taste for salt and also paprika, adding more if you want it to be smokier. Season with freshly ground pepper.

3. Lay the salmon in the soup, cover, and cook 5 minutes longer. Serve yourself a bowl and sprinkle with the remaining parsley mixture and an extra shot of pepper.

BLUE CHEESE SAUCE

This is a universal sauce, pure comfort food and anything but bland. Toss it with pasta, spoon it over a baked potato or polenta, use it generously with steamed broccoli or cauliflower, or more modestly with a steak. You don't need measurements to make this sauce, but it goes something like this.

Put 4 or 5 tablespoons crème fraîche or cream in a small skillet and crumble in about the same amount of blue cheese. Your cheese might be Gorgonzola, Roquefort, Maytag, or a chunk of Point Reyes Blue. All will work. Heat the cream—add a sliver of garlic if you wish—and mash the cheese with the back of a spoon until it melts into the cream. Season with freshly ground pepper. It probably won't need salt. That's it.

If you made more than you can eat in a sitting, refrigerate the leftover. It will congeal but will return to its sauce-like consistency when reheated. As for appearances, the more blue veining in the cheese, the dingier the sauce will look, turning bluish-grey. If it matters to you, chopped parsley can brighten its appearance.

POLENTA WITH BLUE CHEESE SAUCE

Make soft polenta (page 64). Scoop a portion onto your plate or into a bowl, then use the back of a spoon to make a little depression. Pour the blue cheese sauce into the depression, then sprinkle on a few pinches of finely chopped parsley and plenty of freshly ground black pepper. Crown it all with crisp and crunchy golden breadcrumbs, the same ones that go into the omelet with crunchy buttered breadcrumbs (page 160).

Imagine that you feel like something soothing for dinner, but something that's on the sweet side. You're not going to make a cake, but you might make a rice pudding. And if you have leftover white rice, you can make this pretty and unusual dessert. It's flavored (and stained) with saffron, spiced with cardamom, and dusted with green pistachio nuts.

1 cup cooked rice (page 222)

3/4 cup milk

a small handful of golden raisins or other dried fruit, such as cherries

a pinch of saffron threads

2 pinches of ground cardamom

honey to taste

tiny pinch of salt

chopped pistachio nuts

1. Put the rice in a small pan with the milk and raisins or other dried fruit. Bring just to a boil, then lower the heat. While the rice is gently simmering, add the saffron threads, cardamom, honey, and salt. Cook until most of the milk has been absorbed, 10 to 15 minutes.

2. Transfer the rice to a pretty bowl, drizzle on a little more honey, and garnish it with the chopped pistachio nuts. If your rice absorbed all the milk and you want more liquid, add more milk or consider adding a few spoonfuls of yogurt.

CELERY AND OLIVE SALAD

This crisp, crunchy dish can go from a salad to supper if you added some flaked tuna or salmon, a hard-boiled egg, a boiled potato, or all three. The pale inner stalks of the celery are most delicate. If using the larger outer stalks, run a peeler over them before chopping to eliminate the strings. For olives, use green ones. If you buy them unpitted, make sure they're large enough that you can easily slice off their flesh.

1 cup sliced celery

2 teaspoons finely chopped celery leaves

5 large green olives, chopped

1 teaspoon olive oil

salt and pepper

Toss the sliced celery with the celery leaves, olives, and olive oil. Add just a pinch of salt, especially if the olives were packed in brine, and a little pepper. Toss again and serve.

A GLASS OF ZABAGLIONE

A warm, boozy concoction, zabaglione is usually
served as a voluptuous sauce spooned over fruit.
But some view it as an afternoon tonic. Regardless
as to where it fits into your day, it takes about 3

2 egg yolks

2 tablespoons sugar

¼ cup Marsala

minutes to make and is indeed delicious over strawberries and other fruits.
You can, however, just eat it plain.

For one person you'll want to halve the usual 4-yolk recipe, which is possible to do. If you want less than that, you might eat half and have the other
half the next day, chilled. You can use any alcohol, but Marsala is classic.

You'll need a small pot for simmering water and a bowl that will fit over,
but not *in*, the water or else you'll end up with scrambled eggs. You'll also
need a whisk. Have a potholder handy should the bowl get hot.

Get your water simmering. Put the eggs, sugar, and Marsala in the
bowl, set it over the water, and start whisking immediately. Bubbles will
appear, then more bubbles, then suddenly it will seem as if it's all foam.
Keep whisking and the whole mass will turn to a creamy froth. Draw your
whisk through the bowl and if you see any wine that hasn't been incor-
porated, keep whisking until it is. The whole process should take just
two or three minutes. Pour the froth into a wine glass and eat it slowly
with a spoon.

Spy Girls

always get their fiancés killed
in the very first scene.
a femme fatale can't also be
a loving wife and mother.
So she becomes a workaholic
to get over Steve, Jeff, or Lance,
sliding down elevator chutes
cutting through plate glass windows
carefully cracking the codes of illegal governments
dressed in formfitting rubber suits and blue wigs.
Temporarily blinded with acid spray
and shot through a shoulder and thigh,
she still manages to somersault over the wall
to grab the bars of the helicopter
just as it lifts off
secrets of nuclear fission in a disk
tucked in her lace-up boots,
keeping the world safe
from people just like her.
At night, she dreams of rescue,
of blending in with the crowd
of being one more girl
who eats ice cream for dinner
whose purse is not full of explosives.

—Jeannine Hall Gailey

CHAPTER 9

SKILLET PATROL

What Every Boy and Girl Should Learn to Cook
Before They're Men and Women

> *"It is amazing to be able to customize what I'm making. I can decide that I like corn, so I'm going to add a lot, or I like my sausage cut differently than in rounds. Ah, freedom!"*
>
> —Tom Anderson, *young cook and medical student*

GARRETT BERDAN IS A BUSY YOUNG MAN. "When I cook for myself," he says, "I want something fast, easy, and with very few ingredients. It's all about what I can do stovetop, under the broiler, whirled in a blender, or not cooked at all."

A desire for food that's fast and easy sounds typically American. You might be thinking chili out of a can, a tuna melt, that sort of thing. But here are some of Garrett's top choices.

Rotisserie chicken from his progressive grocer's deli with sautéed kale and soft polenta with Parmesan. (He makes a stock with the carcass.) Cinnamon-scented quinoa with almonds and pine nuts, chili-and-garlic sautéed chard, all topped with eggs cooked over easy. Huevos rancheros with corn tortillas, (canned) black beans, avocado, chèvre, and chipotle tomato sauce. **Frittata with caramelized onions, spinach, and black pepper.** A bag-o-salad (he prefers mache) for a **grapefruit avocado salad** with bacon-wrapped prawns. And finally, a smoothie with hemp seed protein powder, frozen wild blueberries, almond milk, and a banana.

After looking over his list, Garrett adds, "Geez, I think I need to slow down and cook more. I've gone all winter without anything braised. Darn!"

One conclusion we've reached while talking, writing, and cooking our way through this book is that it's good to know how to cook for oneself, and essential for anyone who wants to have some self-reliance in the kitchen and who wants to eat well. Think of Betty Fussell and how effortlessly she throws together her Mexican soup out of bits and pieces she finds in her fridge and what joy it gives her. Or Maureen, who looks forward to the adventure of cooking with new ingredients. And Peggy, who casually roasts a chicken for herself or makes spicy little Moroccan meatballs for her friends. Then there are the food maniacs, like Cliff, who get a wild hair to make complicated little crepinettes on a Sunday afternoon, or Daniel Halpern, who thinks nothing of roasting a leg of lamb for his solitary dinner—and why should he? These pages are filled with people who have something they can cook, like to cook, and for whom the kitchen is not a daunting place to be at the end of the day. Rather, it's a place of relaxation and adventure.

Another reason that it's good to have a modicum of skill in the kitchen is that you might want to share a meal with someone else someday—a friend, a colleague, a potential lover, even your parents. It's fun to impress those who reared you with your newfound skills. And parents would be doing their offspring an enormous favor by cooking good food while their kids are growing up, then making sure that their children learn to prepare even a few basic dishes and have some idea about putting whole meals together.

"The Boy Scouts," one young man points out, "do have a merit badge in cooking." But parents shouldn't depend on the Boy Scouts to teach their sons how to cook. Yes, they have the merit badge, but among its lengthy requirements is not one word about goodness, pleasure, or food being something to enjoy, whether eaten alone or with others. Boy Scout cooking is a sad, dreary document concerned mostly with dietary requirements and hygiene. And besides, why wait until boys are of Scout age for them to start cooking?

To ward off the inevitable questions one can't answer while your teeth are being cleaned, I asked my hygienist to tell me how her eight year old was doing.

"He is so excited about cooking!" she answered. "We have this wonderful program in school called Cooking with Kids, which he loves. I've copied all the recipes from their classes and made a little book for Jared. He cooks eggs and oatmeal for breakfast for himself and his sister, and he helps me at night cutting up vegetables. He's so proud of what he can do. We all love this program."

But there are other aspects to Jared's cooking adventures that don't have to do with actual cooking. "It seems to have given him so much confidence," his mother explains. "When he's cutting up broccoli with a knife he feels in charge, and he feels creative as he tries cutting it one way and then another. Being in the kitchen has given him his own area of expertise that he's very happy to have."

Fran, whose children are long grown, writes that when her kids were ten and twelve, she had them make dinner one night a week. "They had to plan it, buy it, cook, serve, and clean up, but just for one night. On Ben's first night he made French fries out of the *Joy of Cooking*—perfectly," she recalls.

"I just did what it said," Ben explained to his mom, then foraged onward, eventually making crêpes his specialty.

"This lasted only about a year, until the kids were too over-booked," she recalls, "but it made a lasting impression. They're not scared of the kitchen, and they had already learned the hard way that you can't start cooking brown rice fifteen minutes before you want to serve it."

There were some advantages for Fran, too. "I was going crazy every night, coming home late from work and then having to plunge into the big meal, which I usually hadn't even thought about, much less acquired. It took away that stress and I had the delicious feeling of walking into my own kitchen and saying, 'What's for dinner?' But it turned out that the lasting benefit was involving the kids in the real life process of feeding people—it was just invaluable."

Brooke Willeford, a young man who writes dialogue for computer games in Seattle, told me that he started cooking "partially because my parents thought it would be good for me and partially because they told me I could cook whatever I wanted to eat." That can be pretty exciting for a teenager. "There were a few meals of theirs that I didn't much like, but with a few tweaks I could get something I found very tasty. So my cooking started with pulling stir-fried beef out of the wok before the sauce was added or shifting some other portion of dinner into its own pot so that I could avoid some part of the meal that I didn't like."

Today, as the cook in his household of two, Brooke admits that their menus aren't always ideal. With his wife working on her Ph.D. and Brooke working fifty-hour weeks, there's the occasional frozen lasagna or the tendency to skimp on vegetables. "Still," he says, "we do a whole lot better than many of our friends, especially our bachelor friends, who tend toward takeout."

When Brooke finds himself cooking alone, he turns to foods that are as simple as possible—black beans, burritos, and quesadillas being favorites, along with his signature dish: chicken fajitas cooked on a George Foreman grill.

"I like this dish because I've never had a bad batch. I've had subpar ones, but even they taste pretty good, plus it's really easy." Then Brooke mentions other riffs on Southwestern foods and flavors. "I absolutely adore anything vaguely lime-flavored that I can roll up in a tortilla with sour cream, salsa, black olives, Cheddar cheese, and lettuce!" Clearly, tortilla-wrapped foods have become quite unmoored from their origins, but Brooke's repertoire isn't limited to Tex-Mex flavors. Compromise born of the wish to please another has its advantages it turns out. Brooke's wife prefers Mediterranean foods, so Brooke's repertoire has expanded to include dishes that aren't based on salsa, cheese, and beans. But regardless of what he's cooking, he credits those two nights a week his parents had him make dinner for giving him his sense of ease in the kitchen today and his ability to go beyond what he ate as a kid.

Tom Anderson is another young adult who cooks. Credit goes to his mother, Doe, for setting a good table and teaching Tom how to cook.

"I remember noticing when I was in the seventh or eighth grade," Tom tells me, "that dinner at a friend's house consisted of steamed carrots and chicken breasts. It was pretty bland. I realized then how much better a cook my mother was. I think we took it for granted for a long time. But I've noticed it more since going to college and eating dorm food, which wasn't that bad. But let's face it, mass-produced food is nothing like home cooking."

Tom is twenty-three. He has been working in a laboratory in a Boston hospital and will be going to medical school soon. While some kids start to cook in college, for most it's not the moment. School is demanding and kids are busy. "Throughout school there was no time," explains Tom, "so it became a habit not to spend time on things like preparing food. After college and after moving into an apartment, I realized that I had time, but it didn't occur to me immediately to get up from my computer and cook. It wasn't until I saw myself ordering yet another jumbo chicken parm and a jumbo meatball sandwich to eat over four nights running that I called my mom and said, 'I've decided to start cooking. Could I come over for a tutorial?'"

For his first dish, Tom chose to make one of his favorites, a mushroom risotto, while his mother zeroed in on a less ephemeral dish of baked pasta.

"We went shopping, came home, and cooked," says Tom. "We ate the risotto for dinner, and I got to take home the pasta dish. Next we made minestrone, then I made it on my own, only I added sausage and tortellini—it's really thick! It's amazing to be able to customize what I'm making. I can decide that I like corn, so I'm going to add a lot, or I like my sausage cut differently than in rounds. Ah, freedom!" (His mom, however, thinks his minestrone is a little over the top with both ravioli and sausage going in there.)

After a month Tom had cooked the following foods: "Minestrone. I've made guacamole three times—it's my mom's recipe. It's really good. I've made chicken quesadillas eight times (he starts with a chicken breast, flattens it, then sears it), and chicken carbonara once.

That was the weakest. I had more noodles than anything else. The egg was chunkier than I thought it would be, and I didn't have enough bacon and peas. I cooked all the parts myself, but I need to do it again. And I just made the minestrone again. I was amazed. Even shopping at Whole Foods it cost fifteen dollars to make. That's three meals worth—it seemed like a bargain to me."

Even in the face of something as daunting as medical school, Tom plans to keep up his cooking. "I think I can take a few hours off every few nights to do something good and healthy for myself—cooking and working out." And he probably will, because, "One thing about cooking," Tom says, "is that you really appreciate the leftovers. They're so much better than takeout."

Despite the pressures of college, one young man we know bought himself a set of good pots and pans as soon as he got to MIT and is now cooking his own meals. Having been reared by parents who grew a big garden (his mother also had a natural foods café for many years and later founded the Cooking with Kids program), Peer Hofstra is already somewhat proficient with vegetables. Now he's experimenting with other foods. His mother, Lynn Walters, reports on his progress. "Peer called last night and said he'd bought a lamb shank and wanted to know what should he do with it." Another call brought a question about what to do with cured meats and should they be refrigerated or not? Lynn is thrilled that he's trying new foods, that he calls for advice, and that she's able to help, even from a distance. Mothers who cook are a tremendous resource.

Young people who are able to feed themselves are bound to be quite something in the eyes of their friends who don't know how to cook. They will be admired and sought after. More than once we've met a young man who can dazzle his guy friends—and girlfriends—with even a modest amount of kitchen prowess. My twenty-four-year-old nephew cooked his way into a house he wanted to live in by impressing his future roommates sufficiently with a single meal that they agreed immediately he should live there. And Tom Anderson has already shared his new cooking skills.

"I had three friends over for dinner and served a risotto with sausage, artichoke, and peas; a green salad; and a chocolate-peppermint ice cream cake." And he dressed his own salad with olive oil, vinegar, and salt. "That's something I knew from living at home," he said.

His friends were impressed.

Although this menu seems ambitious for one who describes himself as standing on new and shaky kitchen legs, Tom had a theory as to why it wasn't so hard for him to pull off what is a rather sophisticated meal, one demanding last-minute attention to detail.

"Working in labs, as I have for the last three years, isn't that different from kitchen work. It's all recipes. So the multiple things going on at once in the kitchen were never overwhelming. I could make the risotto while prepping the dessert—not a big deal. At one point I was tending all three dishes at once!"

Some of our young acquaintances tell us that they like to go out to eat, preferably with a group of their friends. But even so, there are some dishes that might be good for them to know how to cook, dishes that aren't too expensive that they can share, like spaghetti, or a perfectly cooked pot of rice to put under a curry, or a roast chicken and a well-dressed salad. Having even a few fundamentals under the belt will make a young person self-reliant. And when his friends discover that he can cook, and should they become serious poachers and pests in the kitchen, they might be asked to chip in some cash for their home-cooked meals. Before you know it, that young man (or woman) might have a supper club going.

For some young people, cooking can become an avenue to friendships and popularity when confidence in other areas isn't strong. Bread in its many guises was my introduction to the world of cooking and my means to overcoming shyness. It served as a springboard from which I quickly dove into all the other foods that might be cooked as well, starting with soups to go with that bread.

For others, cooking can be a form of self-defense. My niece, writing from Italy, where she is spending her junior year, described pretty much a starch- and cheese-based diet for the first month. Then she wrote, "My roommate and I are cooking vegetable dinners at home to combat the overwhelming, albeit friendly barrage of pasta and pizza. Otherwise it is possible that I may return from Italy in the shape of a large noodle."

Entertaining is something else a young person might want to take on one day, and there are different ways to go about it. A bachelor I once knew (not a kid but he can be an example to one) was very smart about food and wine. He served beautifully orchestrated dinners that were always flawless because he had just two menus. He made those menus over and over and they were easy for him to produce because he knew just what to expect. For his guests, the meals were always enjoyable to eat because they were so well made. He avoided being a slave to entertaining, yet he entertained with great style. His method wasn't any secret. His friends all knew to expect menu A or menu B, and we all felt lucky to be at his table. So if lime-marinated chicken fajitas are your dish, figure out a few more foods to serve alongside them and stick with that until you want a change. And to stave off boredom, devise another menu as an alternative.

Quite in contrast to the well-thought-out menu approach is a story Eugene Walter tells in the book *Milking the Moon*. When he lived in New York as a young man, he loved to entertain and did so whenever money was available for a party. Once, when the check he was counting on didn't come through but he had already invited people to a soiree, he was forced to work with what he had on hand, which wasn't a lot. So he decorated his table with red crepe paper, put out two big jars of peanut butter, and added a festive array of breads and rolls obtained from a bakery where he happened to have credit. He had red wine to drink and everyone had a great time. The most important ingredient here, though, was flair, and Eugene Walter had plenty of that!

Even though I know how to cook all kinds of things, one of my happiest dinners was one thrown together on the spur of the moment for friends we had run into at an art opening in our village. Because we live in the country and can't just dash to the store, I had to cook from the contents of what happened to be a rather spare pantry. But after a short while, we were all sitting down to a big platter of spaghetti with tomato sauce made from canned tomatoes, which I bolstered with bits of smoked dried tomatoes and a handful of fresh parsley. The simplest food possible, but it was so good and the evening was such fun that I remember thinking in the middle of it all how glad I was I knew how to cook, even if it was nothing more than spaghetti and tomato sauce. One thing I do know is this: If we had had to go out to a restaurant in town, the gathering never would have happened and we would have parted in a haze of promises for a future dinner that probably wouldn't have materialized either.

So what handful of recipes should be included for younger cooks, or those just starting out regardless of age? We thought of foods that are relatively inexpensive, foods that provide a meal you can eat from for a while, and foods that aren't super-involved to make. Actually, this description applies to most of the recipes in this book.

Some foods we think are especially good to know how to make include a pasta you can make from what's in the cupboard; a **green salad**; a **roast chicken** and a **stock** from its carcass; polenta or mashed potatoes to go with it; a vegetable or two; a **frittata**, which is inexpensive, nourishing, and endlessly varied; a **confidence building pot of brown or white rice**; and a vegetarian **stir-fry** and **tofu curry** to go with it. So here are these dishes, many of them tested by young friends who—smartly—have learned how to cook at least a few good things.

ROAST CHICKEN

This marvelously versatile bird may look like a lot of food for one person. But think of it as the stuff of Sunday dinner, Monday's sandwiches, Wednesday's salad, and after that, soup. Ultimately a chicken is a sound investment.

1 chicken, weighing about 3 to 4 pounds
olive oil
salt and pepper

If you've never roasted a whole chicken, be sure to reach inside the bird to take out any packages you find. They contain the neck, gizzard, heart, and liver. The liver is delicious fried in a little butter, deglazed with vinegar, and eaten on toast. As for the other parts, add them to the stock.

1. Preheat the oven to 425 degrees F. First pull out the two big globs of fat you'll find near the cavity's opening, then quickly rinse the bird inside and out with cold water. Blot with paper towels, getting it as dry as possible. Brush the olive oil over the skin, then season the bird well, both inside and out, with salt and freshly ground pepper.

2. Put the chicken in a pan or baking dish large enough to hold it, the breast facing up. (If you're not sure which is the breast and which is the back, look at the legs and try to visualize a chicken standing. The breast will be the plump, meaty side that faces forward.) If you have some string, tie the legs together.

3. Roast in the center of the oven until done, which will take about 1$\frac{1}{2}$ hours for a 4-pound bird. Pierce the area between the leg and body with a knife: if the juices run clear, your chicken should be done. The top will be beautifully browned and it will smell wonderful.

4. Lift the chicken from its juices onto a cutting board or a platter. Slice off whatever you wish to eat—breast meat, a leg, a thigh—and enjoy while hot and juicy. Save the rest, wrapped well and refrigerated. When you're done with the meat, use the carcass to make a stock (page 216).

VARIATIONS

There are hundreds of ways to roast a chicken, as cookbooks will tell you, but here are three very straightforward things you can do to enhance this simply prepared bird.

- Slip aromatic herbs under the skin before roasting, such as sprigs of oregano or marjoram, rosemary or sage, or an assortment of herbs.

- Mince rosemary, garlic, parsley, and black pepper together, then mash in butter or olive oil to make a moist paste. Rub this between the skin and the meat, especially over the breast but also over the legs, wherever you can manage to gently separate the skin from the flesh with your fingers.

- Fill the cavity with halved lemons, garlic cloves, sprigs of rosemary, and chunks of onions.

Sure, you can buy a box of stock, but you can make your own, too, from the chicken you've roasted. Some recipes for chicken stock will ask you to use an entire chicken with all its flesh intact. This is not that kind of stock. Our chicken has already been cooked and mostly eaten, so it's not going to make a rich "chicken soup" kind of broth—nor will there be a great deal of it. But it will make something that will nicely enhance a soup or a risotto.

1. Once you're finished taking off all the meat you plan to eat, put the carcass in a pot and cover it generously with cold water. Bring it to a boil and skim off the foam that collects on the surface, then reduce the heat to very low. Add a peeled, chopped onion, a carrot cut into large chunks, a stalk of celery similarly chopped, a bay leaf, and a sprig of thyme if you have one. Leave it for several hours—I leave it overnight—with the liquid barely moving. It will slowly reduce and you'll end up with about 4 cups of stock.

2. Strain the stock and refrigerate it. As it cools, the fat will congeal. You can scrape it off and use or discard it. If you don't plan to use the stock that week, pour it into one or two containers, label them, and freeze.

MASHED POTATOES

While russets make light fluffy potatoes because of their floury flesh, really you can mash any potato, including sweet potatoes. And since leftovers are useful, you might as well cook at least two big potatoes.

Mashed potatoes is one of those dishes you can make entirely by eye and by taste, enriching them with tons of butter, as is done in restaurants, or a more modest amount.

2 large russet potatoes, about a pound

salt

butter, sour cream, olive oil, or buttermilk (for enrichments)

chopped parsley

1. Peel the potatoes unless they're organic and you like the good flavor of the skin and its flecks in the mash. In that case, scrub them. Cut into chunks more or less equal in size, put them in a pan, cover with cold water, and add a teaspoon of salt. Bring the water to a boil, then turn down the heat and simmer the potatoes until they're tender when pierced with a knife and easy to crush.

2. Scoop the potatoes out of the pot into a bowl, add a little of the cooking liquid—about ¼ cup or more—and mash with a fork or a potato masher. Enrich the potatoes by stirring in butter, sour cream, olive oil, or buttermilk, to taste. Chopped parsley is good, too, and it flecks the potatoes with pretty green confetti, especially when you use a lot. Taste and add more salt if needed along with freshly ground pepper. Mash until the potatoes are as smooth or as coarse as you like.

POTATO SOUP
MADE WITH LEFTOVER MASHED POTATOES

Here's a simple way to make a soup using leftover mashed potatoes. Soften a sliced leek or small sliced onion in 1 or 2 tablespoons butter or olive oil over medium heat with a sprig of thyme, some chopped parsley, or a few fresh sage leaves. Add about a cup of leftover potatoes and enough water or chicken stock to thin them to the consistency of soup. Bring to a boil, then simmer for about 10 minutes. Taste for salt, season with pepper, and serve alone or with any of the following—a smidgen of cream, a bit of butter or crème fraîche swirled in, chopped herbs on top, or chive butter (page 122). Other garnishes might include slivered arugula, diced fresh tomatoes in summer, or chopped sorrel leaves in spring.

MASHED POTATO CAKES

Reheated mashed potatoes are never as good as they were the first time around, but you can use leftovers to make a really tasty potato cake. The simplest thing to do is to shape leftover mashed potatoes into a patty and brown it in butter or oil. But you might as well take advantage of their neutrality and add, before frying, such tasty bits as sliced scallions or finely diced onions that have been sautéed in butter or oil for a few minutes to remove their raw edge. You can also add grated cheese and cooked greens, such as chard, spinach, or kale, with or without the onions and cheese. For a crunchy surface, press the potato cake into sesame seeds, breadcrumbs, or chopped nuts before frying.

SIMPLE STIR-FRY OF SHIITAKE MUSHROOMS, SNOW PEAS, AND TOFU

Dried shiitake mushrooms are something you can have in your cupboard ready to use whenever you are. But you can also use fresh ones. The dried ones need to soak for 15 minutes, but that's just long enough to gather your ingredients. A dark, toasted oil, whether sesame or peanut, adds flavor to the dish. If you're reheating rice, use half the mushroom soaking water as the liquid.

4 dried shiitake mushrooms

⅓ carton soft tofu, drained and cut into
    1-inch cubes

2 fat scallions, including a little of the
    green, sliced about ¼ inch thick

1 good handful (about a cup) of sugar
    snap peas

fresh or leftover rice (page 222)

1 tablespoon roasted sesame or peanut oil

2 teaspoons minced ginger

1 clove star anise

salt

1 tablespoon soy sauce mixed with
    ½ teaspoon brown sugar

toasted cashews or almonds for garnish

1. Cover the mushrooms with ½ cup boiling water and set aside for 15 minutes. Make sure that they're submerged. While they're soaking, prepare the tofu and scallions and string the peas. Cut several of the fatter pea pods in half lengthwise to expose the little peas inside. Once the mushrooms have soaked, squeeze out the liquid (but don't throw it out), cut away the tough stems, then thinly slice the caps.

2. Cook brown or white rice according to the recipe, or if using leftover rice, put it in a small saucepan and set it over medium heat with half the mushroom soaking water. Cover, and heat through.

3. Put an 8-inch skillet over high heat. Wait until it sizzles when you add a drop of water, then add the oil, ginger, and star anise. Stir-fry for 1 minute, then add the scallions; stir-fry 30 seconds more and add 2 tablespoons of the mushroom soaking liquid. When that cooks off, add the tofu and sprinkle it with salt (yes, even though you're going to add soy sauce), and 2 more tablespoons mushroom liquid. Cook on high heat for two minutes, jerking the pan frequently to turn the tofu. Add the peas, cook 1 minute, and then pour over the soy sauce–sugar mixture and cook, again jerking the pan so that everything is coated and the sauce has mostly evaporated.

4. By now the rice should be hot. Mound the rice on a plate and add the vegetables. Garnish with cashews.

CONFIDENCE-BUILDING BROWN OR WHITE RICE

MAKES 2 CUPS

It's good to know that you can always make rice that will be perfectly
cooked, that is neither crunchy (undercooked) nor mushy (overcooked).

Brown rice: The dense short grains of brown
rice take longer to cook than any other kind,
but if you are a fan of its clean flavor and
chewy texture, you know it's worth it. Cooked

1 cup short-grain brown rice

2 cups water

³⁄₈ teaspoon salt

brown rice can be reheated and it won't break down. It's strong and good
and will wait for you to use it over several days, should you have leftovers.
The one thing you really do need is a saucepan with a tight-fitting lid.

Rinse the rice and put it in a saucepan with the water and salt. Bring it to
a boil, then cover the pot and turn the heat to low. Cook for 40 minutes
without peeking or poking at it. Remove the lid and taste a grain. If you
don't think it's done but all the water has been absorbed (this can happen at high altitudes where water boils at a lower temperature, or it can
happen if the heat was too high and you boiled away a lot of the water
early on), sprinkle 4 tablespoons water over the rice, return the lid, and
cook another ten minutes. It should be done. If not, repeat until it is.

White rice: Basmati rice has its own rules—it gets soaked so that the final grains are long and separate. But all other white rice gets cooked like this:

2 cups **water**

1 cup **white rice**

3/8 teaspoon **salt**

Bring the water to a boil, pour in the rice, and add salt. Return the water to a boil, then turn the heat to low, cover the pot, and cook until the water is absorbed, about 15 minutes, although that will depend on your pan, the heat, and altitude. Try to resist peeking until at least 12 minutes have passed. When the rice seems done and most all of the water has been absorbed, turn off the heat and let the rice steam for 10 minutes before serving.

TUNES

Because I've always found that a partial can of coconut milk or an unused block of tofu invariably spoils before it's used, I suggest using the whole can and all the tofu to make two generous portions to eat over the course of a few days. For ease, get everything together before you start cooking. You can cook the entire dish in one 10-inch nonstick skillet. If you don't have all those aromatic spices in your cupboard, you can make do with 2 teaspoons curry powder. Serve with brown or white rice.

1 carton firm tofu, packed in water

4 teaspoons roasted sesame oil, divided

salt and pepper

3 carrots, peeled and thinly sliced

3 fat scallions, including some of the green, sliced diagonally

1 heaping tablespoon chopped ginger

1 garlic clove, minced

1 jalapeño chile, seeded and diced

aromatics: 1 teaspoon curry powder, $\frac{1}{2}$ teaspoon turmeric, a pinch of ground cloves, $\frac{1}{8}$ teaspoon ground cardamom, and 1 cinnamon stick

1 (15-ounce) can coconut milk

a few tablespoons chopped cilantro

1 cup frozen peas

soy sauce or tamari

1. Drain the tofu and cut it into 1-inch cubes. Heat a nonstick skillet, add 2 teaspoons of the oil, then the tofu. Cook over medium heat, occasionally giving the pan a shake, until the tofu is pale gold. Season it with salt and freshly ground pepper and remove it to a plate.

2. Return the pan to the stove and add the remaining oil. When it's hot, add the carrots and stir-fry over high heat for about 2 minutes, then add the scallions, ginger, garlic, chile, all the spices, and the coconut milk. Season with $\frac{1}{2}$ teaspoon salt.

3. Bring to a simmer and add the tofu, cilantro, and peas. Simmer until the tofu and peas are heated through, about 5 minutes. Taste the sauce and season with soy sauce or tamari. Serve over rice.

SKILLET CHEESE

Think of this as a vegetarian steak, that is, a solid piece of protein that cooks with as little fuss as its meaty equivalent. The cooked cheese holds its shape, gains a golden crust, and turns soft and irresistible. Add fragrant ground pepper and a wedge of lemon, or sprinkle it with dried oregano and red pepper flakes. Drizzle over a spoonful of salsa verde (page 185) or serve with tomato sauce (page 230). Some suitable cheeses are halloumi, caciocavallo, provolone, queso blanco, and firm, not fresh, mozzarella.

4 ounces of one of the suggested cheeses
olive oil

Slice the cheese into rounds or slabs about ½ inch thick. Film a skillet with olive oil, and when hot, but quite short of smoking, add the cheese. Turn the heat to medium-low and when the cheese begins to soften and the bottom is golden, after a few minutes, turn and cook the second side until warm and soft. Serve right away with a salad and any of the suggested accompaniments.

Just about the easiest way to dress a salad for yourself is the way Tom Anderson's mother taught him to dress the salad for the family dinner. Start with fresh, vibrant greens—a single kind of lettuce, a mixture of lettuces, pungent spicy greens, or spinach. First wash and dry them well. Toss them with a few pinches of salt, then drizzle over enough olive oil to coat them lightly after turning them gently many times in your hands. Start with a "capful" of oil, which is a teaspoon or so, then add more if it feels too dry. Once you have the oil on the leaves, sprinkle over about a third as much vinegar or lemon juice; toss again and taste. If you want more tartness, add more lemon or vinegar. If it's too tart, add more oil.

SALAD DRESSING TO LAST ALL WEEK

You can use this dressing over the course of four or five days, and because it's shaken in a jar, you can have more going on than just oil and vinegar or lemon. It does lose its vitality, however, so you're best off if you make just enough for four or five salads, then make a new batch.

1 garlic clove, slivered

3 tablespoons red wine vinegar
  or white wine vinegar

1/2 cup extra-virgin olive oil

1 teaspoon mustard

salt

freshly ground pepper

Put the garlic, vinegar, oil, and mustard in a jar with 1/8 teaspoon salt and some freshly ground pepper. Screw on the lid. Shake well. Taste, preferably on a lettuce leaf, and adjust for oil or vinegar and, of course, add more salt if needed. After the first day, scoop out the garlic so that the dressing doesn't get too strong.

- Try using different oils, such as walnut or hazelnut, alone or mixed with olive oil.

- Experiment with different vinegars. Sweet balsamic vinegar and rice wine vinegar aren't very acidic, so expect to use more in a dressing. Fresh lemon juice and sherry vinegar are more acidic so expect to use less. Aged red wine vinegar is also strong and often very flavorful. Herb-infused vinegars lend their particular herbal notes, and so on.

- If you like Worcestershire sauce in your dressing, add a few shakes from the bottle. For another strong flavor, whisk a teaspoon of mustard into the vinegar. Shake especially well.

- Include a diced shallot in the dressing, but it will lose its sparkle after a day or so. Scoop it out if you like, or leave it in.

- On any day, add fresh chopped herbs, such as parsley, chives, basil, or dill.

- On the last day, add sour cream or blue cheese crumbles.

AVOCADO AND GRAPEFRUIT SALAD
WITH GREENS AND WALNUTS

There's nothing new about putting avocado and grapefruit together, but like many familiar foods, it's a combination that can be overlooked in favor of the new. What's especially nice about this salad besides that it's good (and pretty) is that it gives you a fruit, a vegetable, and a nut all at once. Garrett Berdan adds bacon-wrapped shrimp to his, and pickled onion rings (page 95) are good here too. You could slip a sectioned blood orange into the mix, and add pieces of Manouri or feta cheese. But for now, here's the walnut version.

3 walnuts, freshly cracked, or ¼ cup walnut pieces

1 pink grapefruit

2 teaspoons white wine vinegar

salt and pepper

1 small shallot or 2 scallions, the white parts, finely diced

4 teaspoons walnut oil or extra-virgin olive oil

a large handful of arugula, mixed greens, or the hearts of butter lettuce

1 small avocado

1. Toast the walnuts in a toaster oven until they begin to smell good, 5 to 7 minutes, then remove.

2. Using a sharp knife, cut a slice off the top and bottom of the grapefruit. Stand the grapefruit on a cutting board and slice away the peel, following the contours of the fruit and removing all the white membrane as well. Holding the fruit in one hand over a bowl, cut along both sides of each segment to free them. Let them fall into the bowl, along with the juice.

3. Combine 2 teaspoons of the grapefruit juice, vinegar, 2 pinches of salt, and shallot in a small bowl. Let stand while you prepare the greens, then whisk in the walnut oil with a fork.

4. Wash and dry the greens. Gently tear butter lettuce leaves into large pieces, if using, or leave them whole. Toss the greens with the dressing, then arrange them on your dinner plate. Halve, pit, and peel the avocado, then slice and tuck the pieces among the leaves so that they intermingle with the grapefruit sections. Finally add the walnuts and some freshly ground pepper. (Be sure to drink the rest of the grapefruit juice.)

A SIMPLE TOMATO SAUCE
FOR SPAGHETTI AND MORE

This basic tomato sauce is our answer to the bottled stuff, which never fails to disappoint. You can make a few cups with ease and use it with spaghetti, polenta, meatballs, on pizza, over an English muffin, and in countless other ways. Since worthy fresh tomatoes are expensive and of short seasonal duration, I suggest using canned. One 28-ounce can of crushed tomatoes in sauce makes a deep red sauce, enough for 1 to 1$\frac{1}{2}$ pounds of pasta.

2 to 4 tablespoons olive oil, or olive oil and butter mixed

1 small onion, finely diced

1 (28-ounce) can crushed tomatoes in sauce

1 garlic clove, crushed

salt and pepper

Heat the oil in a skillet—one with high, sloping sides is ideal—over medium-low heat. Add the onion and cook slowly for 12 to 15 minutes, stirring occasionally until it is soft and nicely browned. Add the tomatoes, with their sauce, and the garlic, season with $\frac{1}{2}$ teaspoon salt, and cook gently, stirring occasionally, for at least 30 minutes. Taste for salt and season with freshly ground pepper.

VARIATIONS

There are many ingredients you can use to influence a tomato sauce, such as dried mushrooms, finely diced carrots and celery, and herbs. For example, add one of the following to the onions as they cook:

- 2 teaspoons minced fresh rosemary

- 3 teaspoons fresh marjoram or oregano, or 1 teaspoon dried

- A handful of fresh basil leaves, rinsed, then torn or chopped

---

SPAGHETTI FOR A CROWD

If you have some fresh basil, tear a few leaves over the top. This is a very straight-forward plate of noodles.

tomato sauce (page 230)

salt and pepper

1 to 1½ pounds spaghetti

additional olive oil or butter, to taste

Parmesan or other hard cheese, for grating

1. Make the tomato sauce first. This can be done well in advance.

2. Bring a large pot of water to a boil for the spaghetti. Add several teaspoons salt, then the pasta. Boil until it is al dente—the package will suggest how long, but be sure to taste because at high altitudes it will take longer. Drain, but don't rinse the pasta. Put it right into a big, warm bowl. Toss it with a few tablespoons olive oil or butter, then with the sauce. Taste for salt, season with pepper, and grate cheese over all.

SPAGHETTI FOR ONE

Cook as much pasta as you think you'll eat. Four ounces will feed a hungry fellow. Two or three ounces are adequate for most others. Boil and drain, then toss with sauce to your taste, ½ cup or more.

This is for one hearty solitary eater, but Brooke Willeford claims you can expand it indefinitely. Chicken tenders work perfectly for this dish. Otherwise, get a small chicken breast and slice it into strips. If you want the kind of fajitas you get in a restaurant, add a sliced bell pepper to the onion. There will be extra beans, but you can eat them a second time in a bean burrito or turn them into a black bean soup.

1 chicken breast, sliced into ½-inch strips, or chicken tenders, about 5 ounces

2 tablespoons fresh lime juice

1 tablespoon olive oil

¼ teaspoon dried oregano

salt and pepper

1 (15-ounce) can of black beans, preferably organic, drained, and rinsed

1 jalapeño pepper, seeded and diced

3 tablespoons chopped cilantro

smoked hot paprika or puréed chipotle chiles

½ onion, sliced into ½-inch rounds

2 wheat tortillas

condiments: salsa, sour cream, roasted green chiles, grated Cheddar or Jack cheese, sliced olives, shredded romaine lettuce

1. Put the chicken in a shallow bowl and toss with the lime juice, oil, the oregano rubbed between your fingers, ¼ teaspoon salt, and plenty of freshly ground pepper. Set it aside to marinate for at least 15 minutes, or longer, in the refrigerator. (Left overnight, it will turn a little too soft due to the tenderizing effect of the lime juice.)

2. Meanwhile, heat the beans with the jalapeño and cilantro. Add water to loosen the mixture and season it with salt and smoked paprika or puréed chipotle chiles, to taste.

3. Heat a cast-iron skillet and, when it's good and hot, add the onion and a smidgen of oil. Cook over high heat, turning frequently until wilted and seared, about 5 minutes, then add the chicken along with the juices in the bowl. Cook, turning frequently until the chicken is nicely colored and done inside, about 10 minutes in all. (Cut a piece open to make sure it's not pink.)

4. Heat the tortillas in a dry, hot skillet, then lay them on a plate; add the chicken and onions along with whatever condiments you desire. The beans can go on the tortilla or alongside. Brooke's advice is to put grated cheese between the warm tortilla and the chicken and/or beans so that it melts.

TURNING LEFTOVER BEANS INTO A SOUP

The black beans from the fajitas will be full of flavor, so all you need to do is to heat them with enough liquid—water or chicken stock—to get the right consistency. Purée some or all of the beans to give the soup body and serve it with a spoonful of sour cream and some freshly chopped cilantro on top. Grate a little cheese over it and warm a tortilla to go alongside.

SPINACH AND CARAMELIZED ONION FRITTATA WITH GOAT CHEESE AND A VINEGAR GLAZE

Cooking vinegar with butter over a high heat for a few seconds makes a piquant sauce that sharpens all the elements in Garrett's big-flavored frittata. It will serve two light eaters or provide dinner and lunch for one. During the 15 minutes it takes for the onions to caramelize, you can wash the spinach, crack the eggs, and even make yourself a salad.

5 teaspoons butter, in all

1 large onion, thinly sliced

salt and pepper

½ bunch spinach leaves, stems lobbed off, leaves washed

3 or 4 large eggs

2 to 3 tablespoons fresh goat cheese

a generous splash of balsamic vinegar, or a bit more than a tablespoon

1. Melt half the butter in an 8-inch skillet. Once it foams, add the onion and start it cooking over medium-high heat for the first 5 minutes, flipping or stirring often so that it colors but doesn't burn. Turn the heat down to low and cook slowly, stirring occasionally for another 5 minutes. Add a few pinches of salt, a tablespoon of water, and cover the pan. Cook until the onions are limp and golden and smell irresistible, about 5 minutes longer.

2. While the onion is cooking, wash the spinach leaves, but don't dry them. Once the onions are done, add the spinach to the pan. Raise the heat and cook a few minutes until wilted. Remove the pan from the heat and season with a few pinches salt and freshly ground pepper.

3. Beat the eggs with a tablespoon of water, $\frac{1}{4}$ teaspoon salt, and plenty of freshly ground pepper, then stir in the vegetables and goat cheese. Return the pan to the stove over medium heat and add 2 teaspoons butter. When it foams, pour the egg mixture into the pan and give the pan a scoot to make sure things are more or less evenly distributed. Turn down the heat and shake the pan again to make sure nothing is sticking. Cook until the bottom and most of the top is set. Slide a rubber spatula around and under the frittata and ease it onto a plate. Place the frying pan over the uncooked side, grab the plate and pan and flip the whole thing over. Cook for one minute to set the second side, then slide onto a plate.

4. Return the pan to the stove and turn the heat to high. Add the last bit of butter, let it melt, then add the vinegar. Stand back—the fumes will be strong! Let the vinegar and butter sizzle together while you let it flow this way and that over the surface of the pan. After about 45 seconds, pour it over the frittata. Enjoy it hot from the pan, or tepid.

CHAPTER 10

Meals with a Motive

"Men, do yourself a favor and have more than one menu that you can execute, and let the seduction phase include more than a steak dinner and a bagel for breakfast."

—Peggy Knickerbocker, *writer*

WHILE WE MAY EAT ALONE AND EVEN ENJOY IT, there are times when we don't want to sleep alone and times when we have someone in mind to sleep with. That's when there's a motive to the menu, and what's amazing is that suddenly those who have been otherwise happy eating cottage cheese have a pretty good idea of what makes a better menu for seduction—and even how to cook it.

Peggy Knickerbocker observes that most men have two dishes—one to get her in the sack and one for the next morning.

"And that may be all the repertoire he thinks he needs," she says, "but I can give the man a hint or two: Women are very impressed when a man can cook, and especially when he can cook well. For one, it shows a desirable trait for domesticity. And a man looks attractive moving confidently around his kitchen. So, men, do yourselves a favor and have more than one menu that you can execute, and let the seduction phase include more than a steak dinner and a bagel for breakfast. There can be many menus. For the same woman."

Men *do* look great moving around the kitchen with purpose and a measure of skill, and we are impressed when a man can—and does—cook. It shows there's another side to him, one you haven't met yet. Plus, real cooking, as distinct from opening something and shoving it in a microwave, is an activity that involves all the senses for the purpose of delighting all the senses, and what could be better than that?

"You have to finish with a piece of meat, preferably something you pick up and lick," says the male author of this menu. "But you have to have some foreplay, too. Risotto for a first course—you have to have courses. You can make risotto with whatever you have. I like butternut squash."

So far, so good. Courses are important. You don't want to rush things, and producing a series of dishes says that here's a man who's mature enough to go slowly. "And," our seducer adds, "risotto alone is a slow dish that takes lots of stirring and gives time for sipping and anticipation."

"So, here we go," he continues. "She's here. It's nice to start with a cold glass of Prosecco—it makes her feel like you're a pro—or Spanish cava. Or we might have sherry with toasted almonds while waiting for the risotto." There's nothing quite as compelling as the aroma of toasting almonds, or any nut, for that matter.

"But back to the risotto, put some oil and butter in a pot and add chopped onion. The rice goes in. White wine. Sage from the garden and the squash. Stirring is a shared experience.

"After the first course, grill the chop and from now on, it's no utensils. Eat the chop and a salad with your hands. Finish with fresh figs. Crack open some walnuts. Aged Gruyère, perhaps a pear."

I'm impressed! Fresh figs? Walnuts in their shells? (He must be from Northern California.) A pear? A silky French butter pear perhaps to set off the embedded crystal nubbins of goodness in the cheese. Fingers move carefully as they pick out the pale walnut meats lodged in jagged shells. Teeth sink into the seeded flesh of the fig. Tongues lick the juice from the pear as it wanders over fingers. This is a very sexy meal.

"But if you want to have sex, you don't want to eat too much," cautions the practical Peggy. "One time I had a boyfriend and I didn't know if we would have sex in the afternoon or at night, so I made a *panzanella*, a bread salad with tomatoes. It's good early or late; to bring to bed or to keep you going."

Another woman made *papa al pomodoro*, a bread and tomato soup, thinking that all foods from Italy were bound to be romantic. But her boyfriend, who later became her husband, always referred

to her seduction dish as "that bowl of wet bread you made for me."
At least it's a family story, and clearly there was more going for this
relationship than the success of a dish. Fortunately, that's often the case.
Indeed, one of the first foods Patrick and I shared was a Thai coconut
soup with the pieces of galangal left in, which caused it to be referred
to ever after as "that wood soup we had when we first met." It didn't
prove to be a hindrance to our friendship, though.

It's important to think things through, including what to drink.

"Wine helps a lot," says a man. "A nice bottle, just the age it
should be. A good pinot—women respond to that. Depends on the
person though. Some girls don't distinguish wines one way or the
other. Oysters. Steak. Champagne can't hurt."

"The person I'm seducing is strongly affected by ale, so that's not
a good idea," another bachelor tells Patrick.

"I want her to be uninhibited but not legless. Big California wines
frighten me. A French country wine with a certain
amount of warmth is better. One from Provence.
With dessert there will be more wine—I'm doing
the left side of the menu first and of
course thinking ahead a bit to
the culmination," he says.
"We don't want a sugary
dessert wine, but perhaps a
Hungarian sweet wine. A
half-bottle. It's got a sweet
edge, but it's been aged.
There's a tradition behind it."
Tradition can be very
seductive. I was a faithful Veuve

Cliquot drinker for years simply because a wine rep had come to the restaurant where I was pastry chef and told us, with an effective amount of emotion, the story of the brave, young Madame Cliquot. Once I heard her story, I wanted to be a part of her lineage and the way to do that was simple: always drink Veuve Cliquot.

Patrick quickly learned of the power it had for me. "I don't have to know how to pronounce it," he says, "I just get the one with the orange label."

"We don't want a heavy meal; we want to have our wits about us," says another. "A nice garlic bread is going to be in there and something a little fishy to start the taste buds. Rollmops, young pickled herring in the sweet pickle tradition of Norway. Not too salty; lovely flavor. The person I have in mind has a sweet tooth. We come to the main course, something meaty, say beefsteak. Filet. It's no good throwing it on the grill. Young ladies can be delicate. The marinade is important—an herby, oily marinade with some black pepper—the aromas are thought to be an aphrodisiac. For a New Ager, incense, but we won't go into that."

Curiously, not one person proposed chicken or lamb for a seduction meal. Perhaps people feel that chicken is too common and too bland, which a good chicken isn't (chicken broth is another matter), and that lamb is too robust, bordering on being gamey. Fish, on the other hand, is delicate, while beef suggests lust. Shellfish is somehow both delicate and lustful. It might have to do with its slippery texture, but perhaps it has to do with the primordial briny taste of the sea. How often people have spoken of being invigorated by the bracing coolness and damp sea scents of salt air. It's powerful stuff,

indeed. Whether foods actually possess inherent aphrodisiac proper-
ties is debatable, but if they seem to, then, like a placebo, they do. Of
course, their power to excite has to begin with something as basic as a
person's likes and dislikes. I can't imagine being charmed by a piece of
rare beef, but a perfect white peach or briny little oyster would have
plenty of allure. It's quite a personal matter.

"I don't understand why some people think things like oysters
and roll mops and other forms of cold fish are seductive," cries Patrick,
who finds such edibles profoundly off-putting. He would not have
related well to Jamie's seduction menu, which is as follows.

"I would have to say oysters, followed by crab, followed by
sushi," she says, "maybe with honey panna cotta for dessert, to keep
up our strength."

"I would *never* suggest sushi," declares another woman, "because
your mouth is full the whole time. That could be sort of awkward.
Sushi is better for a third date."

But that awkwardness could be part of the charm. You'd have
to end up laughing at your bulging cheeks and a too-large dab
of wasabi tweaking your nostrils while effectively destroying the
subtle work of the sushi chef. But why be in a restaurant for a
seduction meal?

Here's a menu from a single man we met in Greece, on a tour
of Chios, where we went to learn about mastic, an aromatic, resin-
ous substance that issues from cuts in a tree related to the pistachio.
"Oysters to start. Fresh fruit wine from Limnos. An average-sized
meal." Then he goes on to include veal, with dried peaches in winter,
or duck with orange. And mastic ice cream with a jam of pistachio or
rose flowers for dessert. "Finish with a liquor for the seduction," he
concludes, "and tell me if it works."

The mastic makes an alluring stretchy sort of ice cream with a hint of pine. We don't really have an equivalent food in the United States that I can think of. Marshmallows maybe, but even they don't come close. For some, the mastic ice cream might bypass the oysters altogether, especially with the addition of rose petals.

Another traveler looks to the oyster for a promising beginning of a far more modest meal. "Start with grilled oysters wrapped in pancetta with a balsamic vinegar sauce," he suggests, "then have angel-hair pasta *aglio-olio*, with long-cooked rapini. Serve up a platter of lemon-seared sea scallops. And after that, a warm **custard** for dessert with **shortbread**."

The warm custard makes a brilliant finish for this menu. Soft, silky eggs and cream, such primitive stuff to fall into. The land equivalent of shellfish. The shortbread offers just enough crunch to keep things lively, but the pieces need to be tiny, our friend advises, or they'll be too filling. Besides, any leftovers will be great for breakfast the next morning, along with the custard.

Egg dishes, especially custards and soufflés, do strike a primal note and they come up often. When I took my twenty-year-old niece, Lindsay, to dinner at Chez Panisse, we were invited to eat in the kitchen, which gave us a chance to chat with the cooks and waiters as we ate and they worked. During the lull between seatings, Phillip Dedlow, one of the cooks, said to Lindsay out of the blue, "Every girl needs to learn how to cook, swim, and shoot. If there's someone in your life you wish to entice, you might want to make a soufflé."

She arched an eyebrow and I recalled that no one gave me any such advice when I was twenty. (Lucky girl!) At that moment, Phillip was in fact whipping up egg whites for a leek-and-spinach-pudding soufflé that would be served surrounded with sautéed chanterelles and their honey-colored juices. We had eaten this dish an hour earlier and I had quietly nominated it as a seductive one. The eggy tenderness and the fragrant, woodsy mushrooms suggested a blend of comfort that inspired trust, and mystery, which promised adventure.

"So what would your menu be if you wanted to seduce someone?" I asked, hoping that I wasn't violating any unspoken rules.

He considered his options as he folded the beaten whites into the soufflé base, then said, "Oysters. Olympias. They're rare. In fact, the best thing about them is that she knows you had to look hard to find them. You can't just go get them at the store. Then," he continued as he ladled the batter into ramekins while musing about what might follow the little Olympias, "I think a simple, beautiful broth, maybe a chicken broth, because broths are soothing. They're hot and warming, but also light. I might have some pasta in it, some fresh noodles infused with saffron and sautéed woodsy mushrooms, porcini or chanterelles. Then a little hanger steak, plus beef heart, slivered and skewered, a *salsa verde* spooned over it."

Another long pause ensues. "On the second thought," Phillip says, quickly reversing directions, "Let's skip the main course. I'd have pears. Pears are an investment in the future. They take years to mature, so there's the idea there of commitment and time."

It's increasingly clear that Phillip will have to aim his menu at another cook, or the kind of person who knows about growing pears and sourcing the elusive Olympia oyster, who sees the virtue in a well-made broth. No one else had brought up rarity and provenance as part of their seduction menu, but there are women I'm confident this would work for.

"What about chocolate," Lindsay pipes up? She's already asked about chocolate a few times, but Phillip has avoided answering her. Again he ignores her question. The dessert he's dreaming of consists of those pears, or raspberries and figs, with a crème fraîche or honey sorbet.

"But the next best thing," he says, finally turning to Lindsay, "would be a gelato by the Trevi fountain and a little piece of 70 percent chocolate."

I mention that there are no vegetables in this meal, taking, for once, a more sensible tack.

"Well, you can have vegetables in the morning," Lindsay says, "if it matters."

"Chocolate, yes, but the chocolate mustn't be too big," says a man who clearly had chocolate in mind. That, and wine. "A brownie would be too much. More like a mousse, a creamy mousse from a shop. And for wine, the creamiest of cream Sherries with a chocolately color with strength and subtly. A half-bottle. Or a full bottle, leaving half for seducing someone else the next week."

What about side dishes? Everyone mentions oysters and steak, but there are seldom sides, I've noticed.

"There will be sides," an English bachelor declares. "Game chips, which is a potato halfway between a chip (as in fish & chips) and French fries. Just a few of them. The person I'm seducing is a healthy eater, but she wouldn't make steak and chips for herself, so some vegetable has to be in there. It might be a little salad. Watercress. It doesn't interest me, but it has to be there. This makes her feel that I'm not absolutely wicked. And watercress is a little bit tingly and spicy."

Women think about seduction meals, too, of course. A tiny female friend of ours says that she believes, along with MFK Fisher, that things shouldn't get too heavy.

"Start with some **salted, almondy almonds** with a light drink, like sherry or champagne. For the first course we'd have ravioletti with finely chopped greens. I use Swiss chard and sauté it first, and ricotta cheese," she explains. "Make the ravioli no bigger than a quarter. Boil them in lightly salted water and float them in a rich beef or veal stock. Add a little Parmigiano-Reggiano.

"For the second," she continues, "I think **scallops sautéed** and served in a light wine reduction. I like to serve **asparagus** cut on the bias. We'd make that together. Maybe have a little bread with the scallops.

"And for dessert," she concludes, "this gorgeous truffled white cheese with bread. **Fruit in season**—grapes, cherries. We'd feed each other. Beeswax candles lit at the table. I got him!"

Peggy proposes a fish menu, too, but not one that is slithery. Her's has more substance and chew. "I'd do a fish baked with braised fennel, white wine, and olives," she says. "Then I'd give him my roasted tattooed potatoes from my olive oil book. And then I'd give him a wonderful arugula salad with candied walnuts and slivered beets with crumbled blue cheese over the top. I'd give him **wine jelly** for dessert. Marsala in jelee."

The quivery Marsala in jelee is based on a recipe from Peggy's book, *Simple Soirees*. Light, cool, and seductive, it also has a bit of buzz to it. It's a perfect dessert.

A woman told us of a meal she cooked for her girlfriend when they were first getting together. It included oysters and a big steak—they're both Texans—but also contained a little surprise, because the one cooking had done some undercover work beforehand. Talking to the mother of her intended girlfriend, she found out what her favorite foods were, then made one of them as well—shrimp remoulade. It made a lasting—an effective—impression that she had taken that extra step to surprise her lover with her secret knowledge of a favorite dish.

Food is used not only to woo someone into bed but into one's life as a new friend, with the possibility of becoming a lover, or not. The food we offer might well lead to marriage, which shows how powerful cooking for another can be.

"The dish that made me *marry* my husband," reports one woman, "was his *mole poblano*, and the fact that he spent days making it. When I got to his house, there was something in the air I had never smelled before. It was utterly amazing!

"But," she adds, "it was also a high-pressure meal. What if I hadn't liked it? I don't know what would have happened. But I did like it. And now he makes his moles in far less time."

This story was told over a dinner with five Minnesotan women I had met while on a book tour. In answer to my question, what would you cook if you wanted to seduce someone, the youngest woman, a pretty blond publicist about twenty-five years old, shrugged and said that she'd have to make her spaghetti with red sauce because that was all she knew how to cook.

"But," her companions chimed in, "cooking anything for someone says that you care!" And the sign of a caring person is no small matter.

A friend of ours was in a professional relationship with a woman for a period of time. When it was clear that part of their relationship should be over so that it might blossom in other ways, he invited her to dinner. But this wasn't merely dinner. It was a meal that invited her into his life.

"I made my usual pasta *puttanesca*," he explained, "but I served it on a large platter. And I cooked a whole pound of spaghetti, which is way too much for two people, but I wanted there to be this feeling of plenty."

Another special touch came with the tomatoes. "There were red and yellow tomatoes, but instead of dicing them up as I usually do, I cut them into fans and lay them around the pasta."

The beautiful presentation, the generous platter that would necessitate the lifting and serving of the pasta, made me think of the Bowerbird arraying his colored stones to attract his mate with the promise of a beautifully furnished home. This meal was a gift, an offering. (And it did work.)

Cooking together also has a seductive power. Maybe it's the nerves, the excitement combined with the chances of colliding into each other while stirring the risotto or opening the oysters. And there's the challenge of doing something together that's slightly tricky, like rolling out long sheets of pasta or shaping ravioli.

"We'd make fajitas!" sparked one of the Minnesotans.

Fajitas? I was thinking of foods a little less prosaic than fajitas, but then she added, "All that chopping and mixing would be fun to do with someone," and I saw her point. You could make fried egg sandwiches and it would be fun.

"Fondue," suggested another woman at the table, her choice for a seductive dish. Curious, because fondue is one of those few dishes that involves cooking and eating at the same time.

"The dipping of the bread, the small amounts," she elaborated, "we'd feed each other bites of the cheese and wine-soaked bread."

"Our first date was a cooking date," Eric says. He's telling me about getting together with the woman he eventually married. "We made a Spanish dish, a lasagna of sorts. It was so complicated. She was nervous—she cut herself twice. We probably should have made something simpler. It took so long to make that we were exhausted by the time we sat down to eat."

The first meal I made for Patrick when I knew we'd be spending the night together was a picnic. We met in Phoenix, where neither of us lived, because we were going to hear Ram Dass speak. To be outside in the warm desert air by a pool in winter seemed so luxurious that it never occurred to me to look for a restaurant. Instead, I made a number of small dishes to enjoy poolside—a lentil salad, a very green tabbouleh with tons of parsley and scallions, and roasted peppers with saffron and olive oil. Patrick politely declined all three. Legumes, onions—even in the form of scallions—and peppers, were the three foods that completely undid him, which, of course, I didn't know, so my menu was a flop.

The first food he offered me wasn't exactly seductive either, but it showed me a caring man. At that time I was thinking about marriage, and my mind was already made up about Patrick. He met me

at the Little Rock airport with a takeout pizza. My first. The smell of the warm yeasty bread and the melted cheese filled his Astro van as we drove off into the night. The pizza was there in case I got hungry during the long drive to his studio-home in the woods. I was touched that he had even considered that I might be hungry and provided for that possibility.

The second offering came a few days later, on the morning of my departure. I awakened in the pre-dawn darkness to the sight and smell of a plate of slithery fried okra. This was not a food to get or keep me in bed, but I thought that it was a bold and curious move on Patrick's part. The way I saw it, he wanted me to become acquainted with "his" food. So having fried okra for breakfast was also a way of becoming more deeply acquainted with him. Have we ever fried okra in almost twenty years of marriage? Maybe once. But we've been known to order it at truck stops, mostly out of sentiment.

When we met, as is no doubt true with many couples, we didn't know each other's foodscape at all. He was a vegetarian. I wanted to stop being one. He was an artist and a Southerner; I was a cook and a Yankee. But over the years we've blended many of our tastes. We've also flipped food priorities. He is no longer a vegetarian while I regard my forays into carnivorous foods as nearly complete. When I asked him what he'd cook for me now, he gave me a menu that was oddly but truly ours.

"I'd have a bottle of Veuve Cliquot," he began. "And I'd wear an apron with bold stripes, something kind of French looking, not some dorky woman's apron or a farmers market apron. I would have prepared homemade **pimento cheese**, and I'd make panini out of that, cut it up into little wedges for the appetizer to have with the champagne. I would explain the Southern tradition of pimento cheese, and I'd read a poem where a man is behind a woman in traffic. He sees her bumper sticker and it's offensive to him. So he gets out of his car and goes to her window, but then he finds her very attractive. They wonder if they can ever be friends. I'd write my version of that poem and read it.

"Then I'd open a Ridge Zinfandel, and I'd cook roasted potatoes with salt and grill lamb chops and cook some collards. In summer I'd cook yellow squash on the grill while grilling the chops. That would be dinner.

"Afterward I'd have a salad of limestone lettuce, and then I'd have fancy chocolates and coffee. And I'd read another poem that I'd write for the occasion."

He even suggested having lots of candles, though he doesn't care about candlelight for himself. But he knows that women like candles.

"And music," he adds. "Some impressionistic classical music. Debussy. Poulenc, but not the choral music. Ravel, but not the Bolero, of course. Maybe some chamber music. I'd have to give it some thought."

This would be a quirky and utterly enjoyable meal, and we would share it with pleasure. I would be amused at the pimento cheese and champagne combination, but know that however unusual, it would be good. We would enjoy every swallow of the Ridge until it was gone. I would smile at his poems, and he'd skip the chocolate. The coffee wouldn't be decaf. It would be a long and delicious evening.

And this means a lot because sometimes food can go sideways when couples do, and it's one way you can tell that things maybe aren't so good at home. When my first husband and I were drifting apart, our cooking for one another was one of the signposts that said the nurture had gone out of our relationship.

"Your food is so subtle," he would say, clearly meaning bland. Then, after asking if I'd mind, he'd dice up a few jalapeños to throw over my goat cheese soufflé or roast chicken.

"And your food is inedible," I thought to myself. I was unable to get down even a mouthful without choking on all those chiles. Every pain-laden bite produced tears.

At a certain point it was clear that we could no longer feed each other. And then, we were no longer a couple, but two single people out in the world once more. In our new lives we were each cooking solo meals, eventually planning a menu or two that might seduce another to join our worlds, and eventually, that happened. Best, we became good friends again. Today we cook and eat together every so often, but when we do, we thoroughly enjoy what have quite clearly become over time, our true culinary differences. Although living in New Mexico has toughened my tolerance for the burn of chiles, my food is still subtle and he still throws chiles on everything. I sputter and cough, and we laugh through it all.

PIMENTO CHEESE

ENOUGH FOR FOUR BIG PANINI

"Mother would take blocks of American cheese, jars of Miracle Whip, and cans of pimentos, sit under the post oaks and grind them together with a clamp-on-the-table meat grinder." That's how pimento cheese was made in Patrick's family.

This version started out pretty much the way Patrick's mother's did, with pimentos and mayonnaise but Cheddar and Jack rather than American cheese. Then, feeling the pimentos were not as tasty as they once might have been, we switched to thick, jarred Spanish peppers and bolstered the mix with smoked paprika, along with plenty of pepper and a little mustard. The resulting cheese, in our assessment, can be addicting, whether on a cracker or in a sandwich.

8 ounces aged Cheddar cheese, yellow, or white and yellow mixed

⅓ cup diced Spanish peppers or 1 (4-ounce) jar of pimentos

2 tablespoons mayonnaise, more or less

2 teaspoons mustard

1 teaspoon sweet or hot smoked paprika

freshly ground pepper—lots

1 sliced scallion

Grate the cheese on the coarse holes of a grater or run it through a meat grinder if you still have one. Stir in the peppers, mayonnaise, mustard, and paprika, tasting and adjusting as you go. Finally season with plenty of freshly ground pepper and add the scallion.

PIMENTO CHEESE PANINO

"Really it's just a grilled cheese sandwich. Warm grilled sandwiches taste so much better than cold cheese on bread." That's Patrick's assessment of this delicious panino.

pimento cheese

two long slices of bread, such as
    sourdough or country French bread

olive oil or butter

Sandwich the cheese between two slices of bread. Brush with olive oil, then grill in a panini maker until the cheese is melted and soft. Slice diagonally into long fingers, put on a plate, and serve as an appetizer for two or lunch for one.

HOW TO MAKE PIMENTO CHEESE

Pimento cheese did not exist in my Yankee family, so at a recent Mardi Gras party full of Southerners, I asked each of them, "How do you make pimento cheese?"

Not surprisingly there were as many answers as people asked. Variations abounded on the cheese/pimento/mayonnaise theme: Yellow Cheddar, white Cheddar, both, or American cheese. Pimentos out of a jar or raw bell peppers. Onions, scallions, or no alliums at all. Mustard in addition to mayonnaise—or not. In place of mayonnaise, one woman used cream cheese thinned with milk. Another added diced jalapeños, perhaps a nod to her new home in the Southwest.

SCALLOPS WITH SLIVERED ASPARAGUS AND LEMONY WINE SAUCE

Once the asparagus are peeled and sliced, this seductive little entrée comes together in just a few minutes. You'll be cooking the asparagus in one pot and the scallops in a pan, then making a pan sauce and bringing them together, but it's not so complicated to do this. It's even less so if one person does the asparagus, the other the scallops. Just talk to each other to get the timing right.

Three golden-crusted sea scallops per person should be enough—they're rich and filling.

12 ounces asparagus

6 large sea scallops

salt and pepper

2 tablespoons butter, in all

1 fat scallion, the white part with a little green, finely chopped

1 tablespoon chopped parsley or chervil

grated zest of 1 (Meyer) lemon, plus juice

splash of white wine

1. If the asparagus is thick, peel the stalks. Don't bother doing that with thin asparagus. Slice them diagonally up to the tips. (If you're doing this well in advance, put the asparagus in a bowl, cover with a damp towel, and refrigerate until you're ready to cook.) Peel off the opaque muscle of the scallops, if any is evident, and discard.

2. When ready to cook, put up to 8 cups of water to boil for the asparagus. Add salt, then the asparagus and boil until tender, about 3 minutes. Drain them just before they're ready as they'll continue cooking in their heat, then return them to the pan and toss with a little of the butter and season with salt and freshly ground pepper.

3. Simultaneously, melt a tablespoon of the butter in a skillet. When the foam subsides, add the scallops. Cook over medium-high heat until golden on the bottom, about 2 minutes, then turn and cook the second side. When done, have one of you divide the asparagus between two warm plates, then nestle the scallops on top.

4. Add the remaining butter, scallion, herbs, and lemon zest to the pan, allow the butter to melt and foam, then add the splash of wine and a squeeze of lemon and let it all sputter and boil. After about 30 seconds, turn off the heat, add a little pepper, and spoon the sauce over the scallops and asparagus. Serve with crusty bread to capture the juices.

WINTER SQUASH RISOTTO
WITH PARSLEY AND SAGE
FOR TWO, WITH SOME LEFT OVER

This risotto doesn't use cooked squash, as many recipes do, but asks you, or two of you, to take the solid, thick end of a small butternut squash and cut it into fine little cubes. It's a little more involved, which is great if you're cooking together, and yields a pretty risotto with small, melting bits of squash among the grains of rice. Risotto is very filling, however, so plan on eating just a little followed by a salad. Any that's left over can be reheated later or turned into risotto cakes.

1 small butternut squash, about 1 pound

5 cups chicken broth, vegetable stock, or water

1 tablespoon each butter and olive oil

1/2 small onion, finely diced

1 tablespoon chopped fresh sage leaves

2 teaspoons chopped parsley leaves

salt

1 cup Arborio rice

1/4 cup white wine

chunk of Parmigiano-Reggiano cheese, finely grated to make 2/3 cup

1. Cut off the solid stem end of the squash, then peel it. Cut into slabs, then strips, then crosswise to make small cubes. A cup is plenty. The rest of the squash can be cooked another time. Bring the broth to a simmer and keep it over low heat on the stove.

2. Heat the butter and oil in a wide soup pot. Add the onion and the squash, give them a stir, and then add half the herbs and 1/2 teaspoon of salt. Cook over medium heat, stirring frequently, for 5 minutes, then add the rice and stir once again and cook until it begins to look translucent, about 3 minutes. Pour in the wine.

3. When the rice has absorbed the wine, add 1½ cups of the heated stock and simmer gently, while stirring, until it has been absorbed. Then begin adding the rest of the liquid, a half-cup or so at a time, until all has been absorbed and both the squash and the rice are cooked. Taste for salt and season with pepper.

4. Stir in most of the cheese and the remaining fresh herbs, then serve the risotto in warm bowls and scatter the remaining cheese over the top.

BUTTERNUT SQUASH FOR ONE, TWO WAYS
(OR WHAT TO DO WITH THE LEFTOVER SQUASH)

Take the round end of the squash that's left over from your risotto, slice it in half lengthwise, and scoop out the seeds. Steam it over simmering water until it's very soft when you press it with your fingers, about 25 minutes. Put the squash on a plate, put some olive oil or butter in its cavity, and season with salt and pepper.

Or, scoop the cooked flesh into a bowl. Mash it with a fork, adding butter or olive oil, salt and pepper to taste, and, if you are ambitious, some chopped herb—again, sage and parsley would be good (and even better if you cook them briefly in the butter or oil first). You could scatter toasted breadcrumbs over the squash or stir in some grated cheese, such as Fontina, fresh mozzarella, or grated Parmesan. This could be a side dish, or even your entire meal.

WARM MARSALA CUSTARD

4 SMALL CUSTARDS, 2 FOR DINNER, AND 2 FOR BREAKFAST

The timing might be a little tricky, but you can hold the warmth in these custards for about an hour by keeping them in their hot water bath once they come out of the oven. But even if they don't get to the table warm, there's something about custard that hasn't been refrigerated that's incomparably exquisite, rather than merely good. There's Marsala in this custard, enough to leave your guest, spoon poised, head tilted, and eyes asking, *what is it?*

1 cup half-and-half

3 tablespoons sugar

3 egg yolks

⅓ cup Marsala

1. Preheat the oven to 325 degrees F. Bring a kettle of water to a boil for the water bath.

2. Heat the half-and-half with the sugar in a small pan, stirring to dissolve it. While it's heating, whisk the yolks in a bowl.

3. Gradually pour the hot liquid into the yolks while stirring, but not too vigorously. You want to avoid raising a raft of bubbles. Finally, stir in the Marsala.

4. Pour the custard through a strainer into a measuring cup. Scrape off any excess bubbles with a spoon, then pour into four small (½-cup) ramekins. Set in a baking dish and pour in heated water to come halfway up the sides of the ramekins. Lay a sheet of foil over the custards and bake in the center of the oven until mostly set but still slightly quivery in the center, about 25 minutes. Remove and let stand in the water bath where they will finish cooking.

SHORTBREAD

This is a simple shortbread that you can make a day or two before your dinner. It won't go bad, though it might get eaten. Make it by hand or with a mixer.

½ cup soft butter
¼ cup sugar
tiny pinch of salt
1 cup flour

1. Preheat the oven to 325 degrees F.

2. Beat the soft butter with the sugar and salt until smooth and well blended. Gradually work in the flour—I end up using my hands—until perfectly blended, then press it into a 9-inch pie tin. Resist going up the sides of the pan more than a quarter of an inch or so, or the shortbread will be too thin.

3. Take a fork, dip it in flour, and press the tines against the rim of the pastry to make a decorative design, dipping it again into flour if needed so that it won't stick. Bake until pale gold, about 25 minutes.

4. While the shortbread is still warm, use a knife to cut it into wedges, then let it cool.

WINE JELLY
(AFTER PEGGY KNICKERBOCKER'S MARSALA JELÉE)

I use Asti Spumate and other sparkling wines to make a quivery wine jelly.

This will give you just enough for dinner plus a little to have the next day.

It couldn't be simpler to make, but you do need to allow time for the jelly to set, so start it early in the day or make it the day before.

¼ cup cold water

1 package plain gelatin

½ cup boiling water

⅓ cup sugar

1 cup Asti Spumate
  or other sparkling wine

2 tablespoons fresh lemon juice

1. Use a bowl large enough to hold at least 3 cups. Put the cold water in the bowl and sprinkle the gelatin over it; let stand for 5 minutes.

2. Pour the boiling water over the gelatin, add the sugar, and stir to dissolve so that there are no strands or bits of gelatin visible. Add the wine and lemon juice.

3. Pour the mixture into a pretty glass dish or just leave it in the bowl. Refrigerate until set.

4. Slice through the jelly with a knife to break it up. Serve it in wine glasses or clear juice glasses. This is a dish where you want to see the light bouncing off all the glistening cubes and chunks of golden jelly. Since you'll no doubt have extra wine, pour a little over the top or into a glass. Serve with something crisp, like shortbread (page 261) or another cookie.

SALTED ALMONDS

MAKES 1 CUP

These crunchy almonds are pretty irresistible, but if you can keep your hands off them after you've had a reasonable amount, they'll keep for weeks in a covered container.

1 cup whole almonds

1 teaspoon olive oil

1 teaspoon sea salt
   or kosher salt

Blanched, peeled almonds will emerge from the oven smooth and golden. With the skins left on, they're earthier, but both are very good.

1. Preheat the oven to 300 degrees F.

2. To blanch the almonds, bring a few cups of water to a boil, then add the almonds and let stand for 1 minute. Drain, then slip off the skins. Blot them dry with a towel before adding the oil.

3. Toss the nuts with the oil and roast on a sheet pan until light golden, about 25 minutes. Stir a few times so that they color evenly. When done, add the salt, and swish them around. Taste and add more salt if desired. As they cool, they'll get crisp.

Today's seductive dessert, even a chocolate one, would probably have to include seeds and bark of some kind, like bay leaf, mace, and peppercorns. One of the best chocolate mousses I recall had cardamom seeds in it—this mysterious aromatic crunchy stuff buried in the silky chocolate—and it was wonderful.

2 eggs, separated

1 tablespoon sugar

2 ounces dark chocolate

2 tablespoons water or coffee

¼ teaspoon cardamom seeds

4 tablespoons butter

cream, or not, for serving

Here's a classic chocolate mousse with cardamom seeds added, but there's nothing that says you can't make it using one of the more interesting chocolates that are available today. Just use one that hovers around 70 percent.

This is too much for two, so portion it into 4 small serving dishes. There can be seconds, and there are those who love dessert for breakfast.

1. Beat the egg whites until foamy, then gradually add the sugar and beat until smooth and firm, but not dry or hard. Leave the whites in the bowl with the whisk.

2. Put the chocolate, water, and cardamom in a 1-quart bowl and set it over a pan of simmering water. Stir occasionally until the chocolate has melted, then turn off the heat and remove the bowl. Quickly whisk the egg yolks into the chocolate, then add the butter and stir until it disappears. If it seems to be taking a while to melt, return the bowl to the pan of hot water to speed things along but without turning on the heat. You don't want to risk cooking the eggs.

3. Once the butter has melted, go back to the egg whites and whip them for a few seconds to bring them back together. Fold them into the chocolate mixture, then divide everything among the dessert dishes and refrigerate. It will set in an hour or so.

4. To serve, either pour the cream over the top so that each bite of mousse comes up with some cream on it, or whip it until it's soft and airy, sweeten it with a teaspoon or two of sugar, and then pile it over the mousse.

A PLATTER OF FRUIT

Fruit for dessert might consist of a single variety—a peach or a pear, for example—or a virtual garden of fruits, put out whole with knives for peeling and slicing. Or a plate might be sparsely covered with individual bites of perfection—a

a ripe, aromatic pear, such as a Bartlett

a few ripe figs

a few small clusters of grapes

a small heap of raspberries

walnuts in their shell, put out with
  a nutcracker

few garden strawberries, a cluster of raspberries, a soft fig, a Pixie tangerine, a sliced apple, a few nuts. Whichever way you go, what matters is that the fruit be as good as it possibly can be, which inevitably means local and in its season. This recipe is a sample fruit plate for late summer.

Arrange the fruit and walnuts on a platter and put out two plates and two knives. Slice the fruit and crack the nuts for one another. Have a glass of late harvest Riesling or Muscat wine, or finish with the wine you had at dinner.

Judith Espinar, who eats and reads in bed with
her cat, is a serious lover of folk art. Her Santa Fe
home is filled with gorgeous folk art ceramics
and bright-colored weavings, and one room
alone is filled with carved wooden saints, or
santos. This is where Judy has breakfast.

"I used to always eat breakfast in the kitchen,
but one day I noticed that when I sat in the room
with my saints, I wasn't just fuelling myself for a
busy day, but something else was happening."

She pauses a moment, feeling for that
something else, finds it, and continues. "It's
funny, but the yogurt seems to taste better when
I'm with my saints. I never have it with anything
but almonds, but if I'm in the kitchen I add grapes
and berries and other things. I don't know why,
but the almonds are enough. I slow down. Eating
with the saints is the best way to start my day."

And having supper in bed with her cat is the
best way to end it.

Our thanks

This book would not have even begun if people hadn't been willing to talk about what they eat when they eat alone. Because this project began as a curiosity on Patrick's part with no book in mind—that idea didn't come about for another decade—the names of our first travel companions and informers weren't always included among the scribbles about tingle and burn spices, the virtues of mastic ice cream for seduction, or how to cook a frozen hamburger. On countless occasions since, utter strangers have piped up with their stories about what they eat when they eat alone, and before we could find out their identities, they were gone. Other times, people whom we know perfectly well but who don't want others to know them, go nameless, or are referred to by first names only. With or without revealing identities, we offer our deep appreciation to each and every person who has taken part in this book.

Although they didn't know what kind of stage they were setting (and might not have agreed to it had they known), we especially wish to thank K. Dun Gifford and Sara Baer-Sinnott of Oldways Preservation and Trust for including us on so many of those Mediterranean safaris where, over long bus rides and even longer meals, the germ of this book was born.

Our warm thanks to Peggy Knickerbocker for her generosity, good thoughts, clever ways with words, and her always appealing recipes. The title "Men and Their Meat" is attributed entirely to Peggy as well as the quivery wine jelly.

Thank you to those participants who are involved with procuring, producing, and raising food; winemakers Robert Brittan and Carl Doumani; cheesemaker Nancy Coonridge; farmers Larry Butler, Ed May, and Carol Ann Sayle; tea procurer Sebastian Beckwirth; rancher Hugh Fitzsimmons and artist-rancher James Turrell; and farmers market leaders Joanne Neft, Amelia Saltsman, and Richard McCarthy.

A special thanks to Milton Glaser for his provocative ideas.

A host of cooks and writers also contributed to this book, and we are grateful to them for their fine words and their recipes. Thank you to Daniel Halpern for his poem "How To Eat Alone," and to Jeannine Hall Gailey for her poem "Spy Girl," both of which speak so aptly to the human eat-alone condition. To Betty Fussel, Laura Calder, Paul Levy, Fran McCullough, Mas Masamoto, Rae Paris, Cliff Wright, Sylvia Thompson, Martha Rose Schulman, Blake Spalding, Joe Simone, Greg O'Byrne, Phillip Dedlow, Marilyn Ferrel, Agalia Kremezi, and Kate Manchester—our heartfelt appreciation. And we especially wish to thank Dan Welch for his unfaltering passion in the kitchen. No one uses more (good) olive oil or has more fun doing so.

Thanks to the contribution of family members Winlfred, Jamie, Lindsay Madison, and Miles Kusch, and friends old and new from every walk of life—John Flax, Harmony Hammond, Emily Hartzog, Sam Harvey, James Holmes, Bill Kissell, Charlie Johnston, Peter Jensen, Paul Johnson, Kim Carlson, Sharon Chase, Rosalind Cummins, Ken Kuhne, Patrick McKelvey, Michael McCaulley, Karen Ransom, Owen Rubin, Maureen Stein, Dru Sherrod, Sandy Simon, Marsha Weiner, Brooke Willeford, and Melissa Williams.

To those who helped to turn an idea into an actual book: we warmly thank our publisher Gibbs Smith, who supported the idea from the moment he heard of it; his staff, who have taken on its production with enthusiasm and good cheer; and Jennifer Grillone for her patient bearing with editorial changes and eccentricities. It's been a rare gift to be able to not only write but also to illustrate and design this book.

We also thank Fran McCullough, who gave *What We Eat When We Eat Alone* its first critical read and a nod. And always, our deep appreciation to our tireless agent, Doe Coover, who manages to make it all happen all the time.

Deborah Madison and Patrick McFarlin

Galisteo, New Mexico

METRIC CONVERSION CHART

VOLUME MEASUREMENTS		WEIGHT MEASUREMENTS		TEMPERATURE CONVERSION	
U.S.	Metric	U.S.	Metric	Fahrenheit	Celsius
1 teaspoon	5 ml	½ ounce	15 g	250	120
1 tablespoon	15 ml	1 ounce	30 g	300	150
¼ cup	60 ml	3 ounces	90 g	325	160
⅓ cup	75 ml	4 ounces	115 g	350	180
½ cup	125 ml	8 ounces	225 g	375	190
⅔ cup	150 ml	12 ounces	350 g	400	200
¾ cup	175 ml	1 pound	450 g	425	220
1 cup	250 ml	2¼ pounds	1 kg	450	230